CHHATRAPATI SHIVAJI

THE RULER MAHARAJ

MR VIVEK KUMAR PANDEY

Made with ♥ on the Notion Press Platform
www.notionpress.com

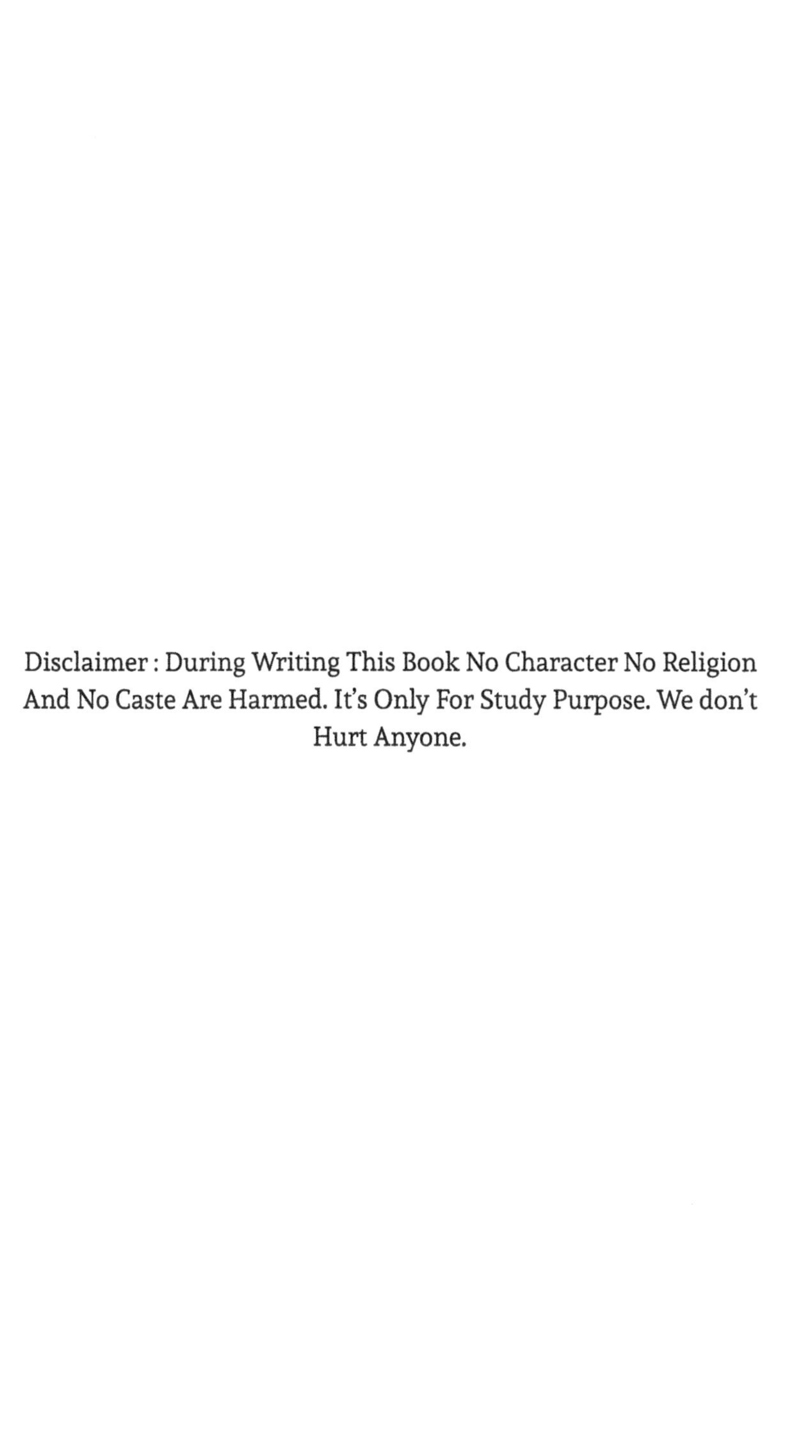

Disclaimer : During Writing This Book No Character No Religion And No Caste Are Harmed. It's Only For Study Purpose. We don't Hurt Anyone.

Contents

Foreword

The Ruler Maharaj Chhatrapati Shivaji Was Born In 16 February 1630 at Kusur. Shivaji Was Indian King & Maratha. We will all know about his work and his empire. During Writing This Book No Character No Religion And No Caste Are Harmed. It's Only For Study Purpose. We don't Hurt Anyone.

Preface

Author biography in English :

MY NAME IS VIVEK KUMAR PANDEY . I WAS BORN IN 30 SEP 2002,I AM FROM SURAT GUJARAT INDIA.MY DREAM WAS TO BE GOOD WRITERS ,MY FAMILY SUPPORTED ME TO SUCCESSFUL AND I CAN DO IT MY SELF.How do I write? That is a question, I believe, that can be honestly answered by me."CELEBRATING YOUNGEST WRITER AWARD WINNER IN GUJARAT 1ST RANK" MR PANDEY JI . I may think I did a good job writing something. The reader is the one who decides the quality of my writing. I do find writing to be natural to me and therefore find it to be a real challenge. My trick as a challenged writer is to do the best I can and know that I am happy with the final outcome. It may take a while to do my best and there may be quite a few problems I run into along the way.

I am not a greedy person those who are thinking about me and my self I never tried it anyone people suffering from sadness ,I trying to get promoted people suffering from happiness and joy in your Life Time. Now in current situation in India and also world people are unemployed and have no many but our indian governor help to people to get free food from ration card , i also take part in leadership team ,i am Motivational speaker , Film script writer. There was my two dream firstly writer and secondly actor & also my own film is upcoming soon i done almost completely completed script for my film .I AM GOING TO SAY WORD OF HEART TOUCH OUT PLEASE READ IT" , firstly i thanks my father he supports me in this field they always getting inspired me by own his words and behavior ,they always said that he was a biggest person in the world in future and also they purchase fruit and chocolate for me in anytime & anyway , firstly my father buy him then call me Vivek you want a chocolate i will say yes papa but how many tell me ,papa: you tell me how much i buy him i told 1 or 2 chocolate but my father purchase whole the boxes of chocolate and they get suprised me.

MY FATHER WAS BORN IN " 20 SEPTEMBER" 1971 IN INDIA.

1) MY FATHER FAVORITE CLOTHES IS KURTA PAIJMA AND ALSO STYLES SHOE

2) FAVORITE SINGER IS KISHORE DA

3) FAVORITE STATE GUJARAT AND KOLKATA , HIS VILLAGE IN BIHAR

4) FAVORITE COLOR BLACK AND WHITE

THEY ALSO LOVE cricket like IPL and one day t-20 .they also like watching a News daily and heard the song daily ,they also interested in tik tok video but in current time tik tok is banned in india but also few videos are in you tube. In lockdown time my family and me very enjoy day daily. my father play daily ludo with his sister and son, daughter.they always loved tea and coffee anytime call me . I make it tea for my father but some reason after the April to june they are suffering from fever and cough , weakness on 6 June 2020 my father death. they not told me say bye bye his life. After death of 6 June on 10 june my mom and dad anniversary.but my father is Best in the world they can do anything for me please take care of father and respect it of your parents.

ONE

Chhatrapati Shivaji

1. Disclaimer : During Writing This Book No Character No Religion And No Caste Are Harmed. It's Only For Study Purpose. We don't Hurt Anyone.

Shivaji I (Shivaji Bhonsale)(19 February 1630 – 3 April 1680), also referred to as Chhatrapati Shivaji Maharaj, was an Indian ruler and a member of the Bhonsle Maratha clan. He initially served as the Jagirdar of Pune after 1664 succeeding his father Shahaji. Eventually, Shivaji carved out his own independent kingdom from the declining Adilshahi sultanate of Bijapur which formed the genesis of the Maratha Empire. In 1674, he was formally crowned the Chhatrapati of his realm at Raigad Fort.

Over the course of his life, Shivaji engaged in both alliances and hostilities with the Mughal Empire, the Sultanate of Golkonda, Sultanate of Bijapur and the European colonial powers. Shivaji's military forces expanded the Maratha sphere of influence, capturing and building forts, and forming a Maratha navy. Shivaji established a competent and progressive civil rule with well-structured administrative organisations. He revived ancient Hindu political traditions, court conventions and promoted the usage of the Marathi and Sanskrit languages, replacing Persian in court and administration.

Shivaji's legacy was to vary by observer and time, but nearly two centuries after his death, he began to take on increased importance with the emergence of the Indian independence movement, as many Indian nationalists elevated him as a proto-nationalist and hero of the Hindus.

- **life of Shivaji**

Shivaji was born in the hill-fort of Shivneri, near the city of Junnar, which is now in Pune district. Scholars disagree on his date of birth. The Government of Maharashtra lists 19 February as a holiday commemorating Shivaji's birth (Shivaji Jayanti). Shivaji was named after a local deity, the goddess Shivai Devi. Shivaji's father Shahaji Bhonsle was a Maratha general who served the Deccan Sultanates. His mother was Jijabai the daughter of Lakhuji Jadhavrao of Sindhkhed, a Mughal-aligned sardar claiming descent from a Yadav royal family of Devagiri.

Shivaji belonged to Maratha family of Bhonsle clan. His paternal grandfather Maloji (1552–1597) was an influential general of Ahmadnagar Sultanate, and was awarded the epithet of "Raja". He was given deshmukhi rights of Pune, Supe, Chakan and Indapur for military expenses. He was also given Fort Shivneri for his family's residence (c. 1590).At the time of Shivaji's birth, power in the Deccan was shared by three Islamic sultanates: Bijapur, Ahmednagar, and Golkonda. Shahaji often changed his loyalty between the Nizamshahi of Ahmadnagar, the Adilshah of Bijapur and the Mughals, but always kept his jagir (fiefdom) at Pune and his small army.

- **Young Shivaji meeting his father Shahaji**

In 1636, the Adil Shahi sultanate of Bijapur invaded the kingdoms to its south. The sultanate had recently become a tributary state of the Mughal empire. It was being helped by Shahaji, who at the time was a chieftain in the Maratha uplands of western India. Shahaji was looking for opportunities of rewards of jagir land in the conquered territories, the taxes on which he could collect as an annuity.

Shahaji was a rebel from brief Mughal service. Shahaji's campaigns against the Mughals, supported by the Bijapur government, were generally unsuccessful. He was constantly pursued by the Mughal army and Shivaji and his mother Jijabai had to move from fort to fort.

In 1636, Shahaji joined in the service of Bijapur and obtained Poona as a grant. Shahaji, being deployed in Bangalore by the Bijapuri ruler Adilshah, appointed Dadoji Kondadeo as Poona's administrator. Shivaji and Jijabai settled in Poona. Kondadeo was tasked with training Shivaji in the administration of the Poona jagir. While Shivaji was quick to pick up physical activities such as wrestling and horsemanship, he was not especially literate and relied on his subordinate ministers to have petitions and letters read to him. Kondadeo died in 1647 and Shivaji took over the administration. One of his first acts directly challenged the Bijapuri government.

- **Bijapur sultanate**

In 1646, 16-year-old Shivaji took the Torna Fort, taking advantage of the confusion prevailing in the Bijapur court due to the ailment of Sultan Mohammed Adil Shah, and seized the large treasure he found there. In the following two years, Shivaji took several important forts near Pune, including Purandar, Kondhana and Chakan. Also, he brought areas east of Pune around Supa, Baramati, and Indapur under his direct control. He used the treasure found at Torna to build a new fort named Rajgad.That fort served as the seat of his government for over a decade. After this, Shivaji turned west to the Konkan and took possession of the important town of Kalyan. Bijapur government took note of these happenings and sought to take action. On 25 July 1648, Shahaji was imprisoned by a fellow Maratha sardar called, Baji Ghorpade under the orders of Bijapur government, in a bid to contain Shivaji.

Shahaji was released in 1649 after the capture of Jinji secured Adilshah's position in Karnataka. During the period of 1649–1655 Shivaji paused in his conquests and quietly consolidated his gains. Following his father's release, Shivaji resumed raiding, and in 1656, under controversial circumstances, killed Chandrarao More, a fellow Maratha feudatory of Bijapur, and seized the valley of Javali, near the present-day hill station of Mahabaleshwar, from him.

The conquest of Javali allowed Shivaji to extend his raids into South and South-west Maharashtra. In addition to the Bhonsle and the More families, many others including Sawant of Sawantwadi, Ghorpade of Mudhol, Nimbalkar of Phaltan, Shirke, Mane and Mohite also served Adilshahi of Bijapur, many with Deshmukhi rights. Shivaji adopted different strategies to subdue these powerful families such as forming marital alliances, dealing directly with village Patils to bypass the Deshmukhs, or subduing them by force. Shahaji in his later years had an ambivalent attitude to his son, and disavowed his rebellious activities. He told the Bijapuris to do whatever they wanted with Shivaji. Shahaji died around 1664–1665 in a hunting accident.

An early-20th-century painting by Sawlaram Haldankar of Shivaji fighting the Bijapuri general Afzal Khan

- **Pratapgad fort**

The Bijapur sultanate was displeased at their losses to Shivaji's forces, which their vassal Shahaji disavowed. After a peace treaty with the Mughals, and the general acceptance of the young Ali Adil Shah II as the sultan, the Bijapur government became more stable, and turned its attention towards Shivaji. In 1657 the sultan, or more likely his mother and regent, sent Afzal Khan, a veteran general, to arrest Shivaji. Before engaging him, the Bijapuri forces desecrated the Tulja Bhavani Temple, holy to Shivaji's family, and the Vithoba temple at Pandharpur, a major pilgrimage site for the Hindus.

Pursued by Bijapuri forces, Shivaji retreated to Pratapgad fort, where many of his colleagues pressed him to surrender. The two forces found themselves at a stalemate, with Shivaji unable to break the siege, while Afzal Khan, having a powerful cavalry but lacking siege equipment, was unable to take the fort. After two months, Afzal Khan sent an envoy to Shivaji suggesting the two leaders meet in private outside the fort for negotiations.

The two met in a hut at the foothills of Pratapgad fort on 10 November 1659. The arrangements had dictated that each come armed only with a sword, and attended by one follower. Shivaji, suspecting Afzal Khan would arrest or attack him, wore armour beneath his clothes, concealed a bagh nakh (metal "tiger claw") on his left arm, and had a dagger in his right hand.The precise transpirings are not recoverable to historical certainty and remains enmeshed with legends in Maratha sources; however, they agree upon the fact that the protagonists landed themselves in a physical struggle which would prove fatal for Khan. Khan's dagger failed to pierce Shivaji's armour, but Shivaji had him disemboweled; he then fired a cannon to signal his hidden troops to attack the Bijapuri army.

In the ensuing Battle of Pratapgarh fought on 10 November 1659, Shivaji's forces decisively defeated the Bijapur Sultanate's forces. More than 3,000 soldiers of the Bijapur army were killed and one sardar of high rank, two sons of Afzal Khan and two Maratha chiefs were taken prisoner. After the victory, a grand review was held by Shivaji below Pratapgarh. The captured enemy, both officers and men, were set free and sent back to their homes with money, food and other gifts. Marathas were rewarded accordingly.

- **Siege of Panhala**

Having defeated the Bijapuri forces sent against him, Shivaji's army marched towards the Konkan and Kolhapur, seizing Panhala fort, and defeating Bijapuri forces sent against them under Rustam

Zaman and Fazl Khan in 1659. In 1660, Adilshah sent his general Siddi Jauhar to attack Shivaji's southern border, in alliance with the Mughals who planned to attack from the north. At that time, Shivaji was encamped at Panhala fort with his forces. Siddi Jauhar's army besieged Panhala in mid-1660, cutting off supply routes to the fort. During the bombardment of Panhala, Siddi Jauhar purchased grenades from the English at Rajapur to increase his efficacy, and also hired some English artillerymen to assist in his bombardment of the fort, conspicuously flying a flag used by the English. This perceived betrayal angered Shivaji, who in December would retaliate by plundering the English factory at Rajapur and capturing four of the factors, imprisoning them until mid-1663.After months of siege, Shivaji negotiated with Siddi Jauhar and handed over the fort on 22 September 1660, withdrawing to Vishalgad Shivaji retook Panhala in 1673.

- **Battle of Pavan Khind**

Shivaji escaped from Panhala by cover of night, and as he was pursued by the enemy cavalry, his Maratha sardar Baji Prabhu Deshpande of Bandal Deshmukh, along with 300 soldiers, volunteered to fight to the death to hold back the enemy at Ghod Khind ("horse ravine") to give Shivaji and the rest of the army a chance to reach the safety of the Vishalgad fort.

In the ensuing Battle of Pavan Khind, the smaller Maratha force held back the larger enemy to buy time for Shivaji to escape. Baji Prabhu Deshpande was wounded but continued to fight until he heard the sound of cannon fire from Vishalgad, signalling Shivaji had safely reached the fort, on the evening of 13 July 1660. Ghod Khind (khind meaning "a narrow mountain pass") was later renamed Paavan Khind ("sacred pass") in honour of Bajiprabhu Deshpande, Shibosingh Jadhav, Fuloji, and all other soldiers who fought in there.

- **Conflict with the Mughals**

Until 1657, Shivaji maintained peaceful relations with the Mughal Empire. Shivaji offered his assistance to Aurangzeb who then, was the Mughal viceroy of the Deccan and son of the Mughal emperor, in conquering Bijapur in return for formal recognition of his right to the Bijapuri forts and villages under his possession. Dissatisfied with the Mughal response, and receiving a better offer from Bijapur, he launched a raid into the Mughal Deccan.

Shivaji's confrontations with the Mughals began in March 1657, when two of Shivaji's officers raided the Mughal territory near Ahmednagar. This was followed by raids in Junnar, with Shivaji carrying off 300,000 hun in cash and 200 horses. Aurangzeb responded to the raids by sending Nasiri Khan, who defeated the forces of Shivaji at Ahmednagar. However, Aurangzeb's countermeasures against Shivaji were interrupted by the rainy season and his battle of succession with his brothers for the Mughal throne following the illness of the emperor Shah Jahan.

- **Battle of Chakan and Battle of Surat**

A 20th century depiction of Shivaji's surprise attack on Mughal general Shaista Khan in Pune by M.V. Dhurandhar.Upon the request of Badi Begum of Bijapur, Aurangzeb, now the Mughal emperor, sent his maternal uncle Shaista Khan, with an army numbering over 150,000 along with a powerful artillery division in January 1660 to attack Shivaji in conjunction with Bijapur's army led by Siddi Jauhar. Shaista Khan, with his better equipped and well provisioned army of 80,000 seized Pune. He also took the nearby fort of Chakan, besieging it for a month and a half before breaching the walls. Shaista Khan pressed his advantage of having a larger, better provisioned and heavily armed Mughal army and made inroads into some of the Maratha territory, seizing the city of Pune and establishing his residence at Shivaji's palace of Lal Mahal.

On the night of 5 April 1663, Shivaji led a daring night attack on Shaista Khan's camp. He, along with his 400 men, attacked Shaista Khan's mansion, broke into Khan's bedroom and wounded him.

Khan lost three fingers. In the scuffle, Shaista Khan's son, several of his wives, servants and soldiers were killed. The Khan took refuge with the Mughal forces outside of Pune, and Aurangzeb punished him for this embarrassment with a transfer to Bengal.

In retaliation for Shaista Khan's attacks, and to replenish his now-depleted treasury, in 1664 Shivaji sacked the port city of Surat, a wealthy Mughal trading centre. On 13 February 1665, he also conducted a naval raid on the Portuguese held Basrur in present day Karnataka, and gained a large booty.

- **Treaty of Purandar (1665)**

Raja Jai Singh of Amber receiving Shivaji a day before concluding the Treaty of Purandar.The attacks on Shaista Khan and Surat enraged Aurangzeb. In response, he sent this Rajput general, Mirza Raja Jai Singh I with an army numbering around 15,000 to defeat Shivaji. Throughout 1665, Jai Singh's forces pressed Shivaji, with their cavalry razing the countryside, and their siege forces investing Shivaji's forts. The Mughal commander succeeded in luring away several of Shivaji's key commanders, and many of his cavalrymen, into Mughal service. By mid-1665, with the fortress at Purandar besieged and near capture, Shivaji was forced to come to terms with Jai Singh.

In the Treaty of Purandar, signed between Shivaji and Jai Singh on 11 June 1665, Shivaji agreed to give up 23 of his forts, keeping 12 for himself, and pay compensation of 400,000 gold hun to the Mughals. Shivaji agreed to become a vassal of the Mughal empire, and to send his son Sambhaji, along with 5,000 horsemen, to fight for the Mughals in the Deccan as a mansabdar.

- **Arrest in Agra and escape**

20th century depiction by M.V. Dhurandhar of Raja Shivaji at the court of Mughal Badshah, Aurangzeb.In 1666, Aurangzeb summoned Shivaji to Agra (though some sources instead state

Delhi), along with his nine-year-old son Sambhaji. Aurangzeb's planned to send Shivaji to Kandahar, now in Afghanistan, to consolidate the Mughal empire's northwestern frontier. However, in the court, on 12 May 1666, Shivaji was made to stand alongside relatively low-ranking nobles, men he had already defeated in battle.Shivaji took offence and stormed out of court, and was promptly placed under house arrest. Ram Singh, son of Jai Singh, guaranteed custody of Shivaji and his son.

Shivaji's position under house arrest was perilous, as Aurangzeb's court debated whether to kill him or continue to employ him. Jai Singh, having assured Shivaji of his personal safety, tried to influence Aurangzeb's decision. Meanwhile, Shivaji hatched a plan to free himself. He sent most of his men back home and asked Ram Singh to withdraw his guarantees to the emperor for the safe custody of himself and his son and surrendered himself to Mughal forces. Shivaji then pretended to be ill and began sending out large baskets packed with sweets to be given to the Brahmins and poor as penance. On 17 August 1666, by putting himself in one of the large baskets and his son Sambhaji in another, Shivaji escaped and left Agra.

- **Peace with the Mughals**

After Shivaji's escape, hostilities with the Mughals ebbed, with Mughal sardar Jaswant Singh acting as an intermediary between Shivaji and Aurangzeb for new peace proposals. During the period between 1666 and 1668, Aurangzeb conferred the title of raja on Shivaji. Sambhaji was also restored as a Mughal mansabdar with 5,000 horses. Shivaji at that time sent Sambhaji with general Prataprao Gujar to serve with the Mughal viceroy in Aurangabad, Prince Mu'azzam. Sambhaji was also granted territory in Berar for revenue collection. Aurangzeb also permitted Shivaji to attack the decaying Adil Shahi; the weakened Sultan Ali Adil Shah II sued for peace and granted the rights of sardeshmukhi and chauthai to Shivaji.

The peace between Shivaji and the Mughals lasted until 1670. At that time Aurangzeb became suspicious of the close ties between Shivaji and Mu'azzam, who he thought might usurp his throne, and may even have been receiving bribes from Shivaji. Also at that time, Aurangzeb, occupied in fighting the Afghans, greatly reduced his army in the Deccan; many of the disbanded soldiers quickly joined Maratha service. The Mughals also took away the jagir of Berar from Shivaji to recover the money lent to him a few years earlier. In response, Shivaji launched an offensive against the Mughals and recovered a major portion of the territories surrendered to them in a span of four months.

Shivaji sacked Surat for second time in 1670; the English and Dutch factories were able to repel his attack, but he managed to sack the city itself, including plundering the goods of a Muslim prince from Mawara-un-Nahr who was returning from Mecca. Angered by the renewed attacks, the Mughals resumed hostilities with the Marathas, sending a force under Daud Khan to intercept Shivaji on his return home from Surat, but were defeated in the Battle of Vani-Dindori near present-day Nashik.

In October 1670, Shivaji sent his forces to harass the English at Bombay; as they had refused to sell him war materiel, his forces blocked English woodcutting parties from leaving Bombay. In September 1671, Shivaji sent an ambassador to Bombay, again seeking materiel, this time for the fight against Danda-Rajpuri. The English had misgivings of the advantages Shivaji would gain from this conquest, but also did not want to lose any chance of receiving compensation for his looting their factories at Rajapur. The English sent Lieutenant Stephen Ustick to treat with Shivaji, but negotiations failed over the issue of the Rajapur indemnity. Numerous exchanges of envoys followed over the coming years, with some agreement as to the arms issues in 1674, but Shivaji was never to pay the Rajapur indemnity before his death, and the factory there dissolved at the end of 1682.

- **Battles of Umrani and Nesari**

In 1674, Prataprao Gujar, the commander-in-chief of the Maratha forces, was sent to push back the invading force led by the Bijapuri general, Bahlol Khan. Prataprao's forces defeated and captured the opposing general in the battle, after cutting-off their water supply by encircling a strategic lake, which prompted Bahlol Khan to sue for peace. In spite of Shivaji's specific warnings against doing so, Prataprao released Bahlol Khan, who started preparing for a fresh invasion.

Shivaji sent a displeased letter to Prataprao, refusing him audience until Bahlol Khan was re-captured. Upset by his commander's rebuke, Prataprao found Bahlol Khan and charged his position with only six other horsemen, leaving his main force behind. Prataprao was killed in combat; Shivaji was deeply grieved on hearing of Prataprao's death, and arranged for the marriage of his second son, Rajaram, to Prataprao's daughter. Prataprao was succeeded by Hambirrao Mohite, as the new sarnaubat (commander-in-chief of the Maratha forces). Raigad Fort was newly built by Hiroji Indulkar as a capital of nascent Maratha kingdom.

Shivaji had acquired extensive lands and wealth through his campaigns, but lacking a formal title, he was still technically a Mughal zamindar or the son of a Bijapuri jagirdar, with no legal basis to rule his de facto domain. A kingly title could address this and also prevent any challenges by other Maratha leaders, to whom he was technically equal. it would also provide the Hindu Marathas with a fellow Hindu sovereign in a region otherwise ruled by Muslims.

The preparation for the proposed coronation began in 1673. However, some controversial problems delayed the coronation by almost a year. Controversy erupted amongst the Brahmins of Shivaji's court: they refused to crown Shivaji as a king because that status was reserved for those of the kshatriya (warrior) varna in Hindu society. Shivaji was descended from a line of headmen of farming villages, and the Brahmins accordingly categorised him as being of the shudra (cultivator) varna.

They noted that Shivaji had never had a sacred thread ceremony, and did not wear the thread, which a kshatriya would. Shivaji summoned Gaga Bhatt, a pandit of Varanasi, who stated that he had found a genealogy proving that Shivaji was descended from the Sisodias, and thus indeed a kshatriya, albeit one in need of the ceremonies befitting his rank. To enforce this status, Shivaji was given a sacred thread ceremony, and remarried his spouses under the Vedic rites expected of a kshatriya. However, following historical evidence, Shivaji's claim to Rajput, and specifically Sisodia ancestry may be interpreted as being anything from tenuous at best, to inventive in a more extreme reading.

On 28 May, Shivaji performed penance for not observing Kshatriya rites by his ancestors' and himself for so long. Then he was invested by Gaga Bhatt with the sacred thread. On insistence of other Brahmins, Gaga Bhatt dropped the Vedic chant and initiated Shivaji in a modified form of the life of the twice-born, instead of putting him on a par with the Brahmins. Next day, Shivaji made atonement for the sins, deliberate or accidental, committed in his own lifetime.

He was weighed separately against seven metals including gold, silver and several other articles like fine linen, camphor, salt, sugar etc. All these metals and articles along with a lakh of hun were distributed among the Brahmins. But even this failed to satisfy the greed of the Brahmins. Two of the learned Brahmins pointed out that Shivaji, while conducting his raids, had burnt cities involving the death of Brahmins, cows, women and children and he could be cleansed of this sin for a price of Rs. 8,000, and Shivaji paid this amount. Total expenditure made for feeding the assemblage, general alms giving, throne and ornaments approached 1.5 million Rupees.

Shivaji was crowned king of the Maratha Empire (Hindawi Swaraj) in a lavish ceremony on 6 June 1674 at Raigad fort. In the Hindu calendar it was on the 13th day (trayodashi) of the first fortnight of the month of Jyeshtha in the year 1596. Gaga Bhatt officiated, pouring water from a gold vessel filled with the waters of the seven sacred rivers Yamuna, Indus, Ganges, Godavari, Narmada, Krishna and Kaveri over Shivaji's head, and chanted the Vedic coronation mantras. After the ablution, Shivaji bowed before Jijabai and touched her feet. Nearly fifty thousand people gathered at Raigad for the ceremonies. Shivaji was entitled Shakakarta ("founder of an era") and Chhatrapati ("sovereign"). He also took the title of Haindava Dharmodhhaarak (protector of the Hindu faith) and Kshatriya Kulavantas. Kshatriya is one of the four varnas of Hinduism and kulavantas means the 'head of the kula, or race'.

Shivaji's mother Jijabai died on 18 June 1674. The Marathas summoned Nischal Puri Goswami, a tantrik priest, who declared that the original coronation had been held under inauspicious stars, and a second coronation was needed. This second coronation on 24 September 1674 had a dual-use, mollifying those who still believed that Shivaji was not qualified for the Vedic rites of his first coronation, by performing a less-contestable additional ceremony.

- **Tanjavur Maratha Kingdom**

Beginning in 1674, the Marathas undertook an aggressive campaign, raiding Khandesh (October), capturing Bijapuri Ponda (April 1675), Karwar (mid-year), and Kolhapur (July). In November, the Maratha navy skirmished with the Siddis of Janjira, but failed to dislodge them. Having recovered from an illness, and taking advantage of a civil war that had broken out between the Deccanis and the Afghans at Bijapur, Shivaji raided Athani in April 1676.

In the run-up to his expedition, Shivaji appealed to a sense of Deccani patriotism, that Southern India was a homeland that should be protected from outsiders. His appeal was somewhat successful, and in 1677 Shivaji visited Hyderabad for a month and entered into a treaty with the Qutubshah of the Golkonda sultanate, agreeing to reject his alliance with Bijapur and jointly oppose the Mughals. In 1677, Shivaji invaded Karnataka with 30,000 cavalry and 40,000 infantry, backed by Golkonda artillery and funding. Proceeding south, Shivaji seized the forts of Vellore and Gingee. the latter would later serve as a capital of the Marathas during the reign of his son Rajaram I.

Shivaji intended to reconcile with his half-brother Venkoji (Ekoji I), Shahaji's son by his second wife, Tukabai (née Mohite), who ruled Thanjavur (Tanjore) after Shahaji. The initially promising negotiations were unsuccessful, so whilst returning to Raigad, Shivaji defeated his half-brother's army on 26 November 1677 and seized most of his possessions in the Mysore plateau. Venkoji's wife Dipa Bai, whom Shivaji deeply respected, took up new negotiations with Shivaji and also convinced her husband to distance himself from Muslim advisors. In the end, Shivaji consented to turn over to her and her female descendants many of the properties he had seized, with Venkoji consenting to a number of conditions for the proper administration of the territories and maintenance of Shahji's memorial (samadhi).

The question of Shivaji's heir-apparent was complicated. Shivaji confined his son to Panhala in 1678, only to have the prince escape with his wife and defect to the Mughals for a year. Sambhaji then returned home, unrepentant, and was again confined to Panhala.

Shivaji died around 3–5 April 1680 at the age of 50, on the eve of Hanuman Jayanti. The cause of Shivaji's death is disputed. British records states that Shivaji died of bloody flux being sick for 12 days. In a contemporary work in Portuguese, the Biblioteca Nacional de Lisboa, the recorded cause of death of Shivaji is anthrax. However, Krishnaji Anant Sabhasad, author of Sabhasad Bakhar, the biography of Shivaji has mentioned fever as the cause of death of Shivaji. Putalabai, the childless eldest of the surviving wives of Shivaji committed sati by jumping into his funeral pyre. Another surviving spouse, Sakwarbai, was not allowed to follow suit because she had a young daughter. There were also allegations, though doubted by later scholars, that his second wife Soyarabai had poisoned him in order to put her 10-year-old son Rajaram on the throne.

After Shivaji's death, Soyarabai made plans with various ministers of the administration to crown her son Rajaram rather than her stepson Sambhaji. On 21 April 1680, ten-year-old Rajaram was installed on the throne. However, Sambhaji took possession of Raigad Fort after killing the commander, and on 18 June acquired control of Raigad, and formally ascended the throne on 20 July. Rajaram, his wife Janki Bai, and mother Soyrabai were imprisoned, and Soyrabai executed on charges of conspiracy that October.

- **Ashta Pradhan**

The Council of Eight Ministers, or Ashta Pradhan Mandal, was an administrative and advisory council set up by Shivaji. It consisted of eight ministers who regularly advised Shivaji on political and administrative matters.

- **Marathi and Sanskrit**

In his court, Shivaji replaced Persian, the common courtly language in the region, with Marathi, and emphasised Hindu political and courtly traditions. Shivaji's reign stimulated the deployment of Marathi as a tool of systematic description and understanding.Shivaji's royal seal was in Sanskrit. Shivaji commissioned one of his officials to make a comprehensive lexicon to replace Persian and Arabic terms with their Sanskrit equivalents. This led to production of 'Rājavyavahārakośa', the thesaurus of state usage in 1677.

- **Religious**

Shivaji is known for his liberal and tolerant religious policies. While Hindus were relieved to practice their religion freely under a Hindu ruler, Shivaji not only allowed Muslims to practice without harassment, but supported their ministries with endowments. When Aurangzeb imposed the Jizya tax on non-Muslims on 3 April 1679, Shivaji wrote a strict letter to Aurangzeb criticising his tax policy. He wrote:

In strict justice, the Jizya is not at all lawful. If you imagine piety in oppressing and terrorising the Hindus, you ought to first levy the tax on Raj Singh I, who is the head of Hindus. But to oppress ants and flies is not at all valour nor spirit. If you believe in Quran, God is the lord of all men and not just of Muslims only. Verily, Islam and Hinduism are terms of contrast. They are used by the true Divine Painter for blending the colours and filling in the outlines. If it is a mosque, the call to prayer is chanted in remembrance of God. If it is a temple, the bells are rung in yearning for God alone. To show bigotry to any man's religion and practices is to alter the words of the Holy Book.

Noting that Shivaji had stemmed the spread of the neighbouring Muslim states, his contemporary, the poet Kavi Bhushan stated.Had not there been Shivaji, Kashi would have lost its culture, Mathura would have been turned into a mosque and all would have been circumcised.

However, Gijs Kruijtzer, in his book Xenophobia in Seventeenth-Century India argues that the roots of modern communalism (the antagonism between "communities" of Hindus and Muslims) first appeared in the decade 1677–1687, in the interplay between Shivaji and the Mughal emperor Aurangzeb (though Shivaji died in 1680) During the sack of Surat in 1664, Shivaji was approached by Ambrose, a Capuchin monk who asked him to spare the city's Christians. Shivaji left the Christians untouched, saying "the Frankish Padrys are good men."

Shivaji was not attempting to create a universal Hindu rule. He was tolerant to different religions and believed in syncretism. He urged Aurangzeb to act like Akbar in according respect to Hindu beliefs and places. Shivaji had little trouble forming alliances with the surrounding Muslim nations even against Hindu powers. He also did not join forces with other Hindu powers, such as the Rajputs, to fight the Mughals. In his own army, Muslim leaders appear quite early. The first Pathan unit was formed in 1656. His naval admiral, Darya Sarang, was a Muslim.

Older Maratha histories asserted that Shivaji was a close follower of Ramdas, a Brahmin teacher, who guided him in an orthodox Hindu path; recent research has shown that Shivaji did not meet or know Ramdas until late in his life. Rather, Shivaji followed his own judgement throughout his remarkable career.

- **Royal seal of Shivaji**

Seals were means to confer authenticity on official documents. Shahaji and Jijabai had Persian seals. But Shivaji, right from beginning, used Sanskrit for his seal. The seal proclaims: "This seal of Shiva, son of Shah, shines forth for the welfare of the people and is meant to command increasing respect from the universe like the first phase of the moon."

- **Shivaji's mode of warfare**

Shivaji maintained a small but effective standing army. The core of Shivaji's army consisted of peasants of the Maratha and Kunbi castes. Shivaji was aware of the limitations of his army. He realised that conventional warfare methods were inadequate to confront the big, well-trained cavalry of the Mughals which was equipped with field artillery. As a result, Shivaji adopted guerilla tactics which became known as 'Ganimi Kawa'. Shivaji was a master of guerrilla warfare.

His strategies consistently perplexed and defeated armies sent against him. He realized that the most vulnerable point of the large, slow-moving armies of the time was supply. He utilised knowledge of the local terrain and the superior mobility of his light cavalry to cut off supplies to the enemy. Shivaji refused to confront in pitched battles. Instead, he lured the enemies in difficult hills and jungles of his own choosing, catching them at a disadvantage and routing them. Shivaji didn't stick to a particular tactic but used several methods to undermine his enemies as required by circumstances, like sudden raids, sweeps and ambushes and use of psychological pressure.Shivaji was contemptuously called a "Mountain Rat" by Aurangzeb and his generals because of his guerilla tactics of attacking enemy forces and then retreating into his mountain forts.

Shivaji demonstrated great skill in creating his military organisation, which lasted until the demise of the Maratha Empire. His strategy rested on leveraging his ground forces, naval forces, and series of forts across his territory. The Maval infantry served as the core of his ground forces (reinforced with Telangi musketeers from Karnataka), supported by Maratha cavalry. His artillery was relatively underdeveloped and reliant on European suppliers, further inclining him to a very mobile form of warfare.

- **Shivaji's forts**

Hill forts played a key role in Shivaji's strategy. He captured important forts at Murambdev (Rajgad), Torna, Kondhana (Sinhagad) and Purandar. He also rebuilt or repaired many forts in advantageous locations. In addition, Shivaji built a number of forts; the number "111" is reported in some accounts, but it is likely the actual number "did not exceed 18." The historian Jadunath Sarkar assessed that Shivaji owned some 240–280 forts at the time of his death.Each was placed under three officers of equal status, lest a single traitor be bribed or tempted to deliver it to the enemy. The officers acted jointly and provided mutual checks and balance.

- **Maratha Navy**

Aware of the need for naval power to maintain control along the Konkan coast, Shivaji began to build his navy in 1657 or 1659, with the purchase of twenty galivats from the Portuguese shipyards of Bassein. Marathi chronicles state that at its height his fleet counted some 400 warships, though contemporary English chronicles counter that the number never exceeded 160. Kanhoji Angre was the chief of Maratha Navy.

With the Marathas being accustomed to a land-based military, Shivaji widened his search for qualified crews for his ships, taking on lower-caste Hindus of the coast who were long familiar with naval operations (the famed "Malabar pirates") as well as Muslim mercenaries. Noting the power of the Portuguese navy, Shivaji hired a number of Portuguese sailors and Goan Christian converts, and made Rui Leitao Viegas commander of his fleet. Viegas was later to defect back to the Portuguese, taking 300 sailors with him.

Shivaji fortified his coastline by seizing coastal forts and refurbishing them, and built his first marine fort at Sindhudurg, which was to become the headquarters of the Maratha navy. The navy itself was a coastal navy, focused on travel and combat in the littoral areas, and not intended to go far out to sea.

- **Mughal–Maratha Wars**

Maratha Empire at its peak in 1758,Shivaji left behind a state always at odds with the Mughals. Soon after his death, in 1681, Aurangzeb launched an offensive in the South to capture territories held by the Marathas, the Bijapur-based Adilshahi and Qutb Shahi of Golkonda respectively. He was successful in obliterating the Sultanates but could not subdue the Marathas after spending 27 years in the Deccan. The period saw the capture, torture, and execution of Sambhaji in 1689, and the Marathas offering strong resistance under the leadership of Sambhaji's successor, Rajaram and then Rajaram's widow Tarabai. Territories changed hands repeatedly between the Mughals and the Marathas; the conflict ended in defeat for the Mughals in 1707.

Shahu, a grandson of Shivaji and son of Sambhaji, was kept prisoner by Aurangzeb during the 27-year period conflict. After the latter's death, his successor released Shahu. After a brief power struggle over succession with his aunt Tarabai, Shahu ruled the Maratha Empire from 1707 to 1749. Early in his reign, he appointed Balaji Vishwanath and later his descendants, as Peshwas (prime ministers) of the Maratha Empire. The empire expanded greatly under the leadership of Balaji's son, Peshwa Bajirao I and grandson, Peshwa Balaji Bajirao. At its peak, the Maratha empire stretched from Tamil Nadu in the south, to Peshawar (modern-day Khyber Pakhtunkhwa) in the north, and Bengal, in the east. In 1761, the Maratha army lost the Third Battle of Panipat to Ahmed Shah Abdali of the Afghan Durrani Empire, which halted their imperial expansion in northwestern India. Ten years after Panipat, Marathas regained influence in North India during the rule of Madhavrao Peshwa.

In a bid to effectively manage the large empire, Shahu and the Peshwas gave semi-autonomy to the strongest of the knights, creating the Maratha Confederacy. They became known as Gaekwads of Baroda, the Holkars of Indore and Malwa, the Scindias of Gwalior and Bhonsales of Nagpur. In 1775, the East India Company intervened in a succession struggle in Pune, which became the First Anglo-Maratha War. The Marathas remained the pre-eminent power in India until their defeat by the British in the Second and Third Anglo-Maratha wars (1805–1818), which left the company the dominant power in most of India.

- **Shivaji in popular culture**

An early-20th-century painting by M. V. Dhurandhar of Shivaji and Baji Prabhu at Pawan Khind.

Shivaji was well known for his strong religious and warrior code of ethics and exemplary character. He was recognized as a national hero during the Indian Independence Movement. While some accounts of Shivaji state that he was greatly influenced by the Brahmin guru Samarth Ramdas, others have said that Ramdas' role has been overemphasised by later Brahmin commentators to enhance their position.

Shivaji was admired for his heroic exploits and clever stratagems in the contemporary accounts of English, French, Dutch, Portuguese and Italian writers. Contemporary English writers compared him with Alexander, Hannibal and Julius Caesar. The

French traveller Francois Bernier wrote in his Travels in Mughal India.

I forgot to mention that during pillage of Sourate, Seva-Gy, the Holy Seva-Gi! respected the habitation of the Reverend Father Ambrose, the Capuchin missionary. 'The Frankish Padres are good men', he said 'and shall not be attacked.' He spared also the house of a deceased Delale or Gentile broker, of the Dutch, because assured that he had been very charitable while alive.

In the mid-19th century, Marathi social reformer Jyotirao Phule wrote his interpretation of the Shivaji legend, portraying him as a hero of the shudras and Dalits. Phule sought to use the Shivaji legends to undermine the Brahmins he accused of hijacking the narrative, and uplift the lower classes; his 1869 ballad-form story of Shivaji was met with great hostility by the Brahmin-dominated media. At the end of the 19th century, Shivaji's memory was leveraged by the non-Brahmin intellectuals of Bombay, who identified as his descendants and through him claimed the kshatriya varna. While some Brahmins rebutted this identity, defining them as of the lower shudra varna, other Brahmins recognised the Marathas' utility to the Indian independence movement, and endorsed this kshatriya legacy and the significance of Shivaji.

In 1895, Indian nationalist leader Lokmanya Tilak organised what was to be an annual festival to mark the birthday of Shivaji. He portrayed Shivaji as the "opponent of the oppressor", with possible negative implications concerning the colonial government. Tilak denied any suggestion that his festival was anti-Muslim or disloyal to the government, but simply a celebration of a hero. These celebrations prompted a British commentator in 1906 to note: "Cannot the annals of the Hindu race point to a single hero whom even the tongue of slander will not dare call a chief of dacoits.

One of the first commentators to reappraise the critical British view of Shivaji was M. G. Ranade, whose Rise of the Maratha Power (1900) declared Shivaji's achievements as the beginning of modern nation-building. Ranade criticised earlier British portrayals of

Shivaji's state as "a freebooting Power, which thrived by plunder and adventure, and succeeded only because it was the most cunning and adventurous ... This is a very common feeling with the readers, who derive their knowledge of these events solely from the works of English historians."

In 1919, Sarkar published the seminal Shivaji and His Times, hailed as the most authoritative biography of the king since James Grant Duff's 1826 A History of the Mahrattas. A respected scholar, Sarkar was able to read primary sources in Persian, Marathi, and Arabic, but was challenged for his criticism of the "chauvinism" of Marathi historians' views of Shivaji. Likewise, though supporters cheered his depiction of the killing of Afzal Khan as justified, they decried Sarkar's terming as "murder" the killing of the Hindu raja Chandrao More and his clan.

As political tensions rose in India in the early 20th century, some Indian leaders came to re-work their earlier stances on Shivaji's role. Jawaharlal Nehru had in 1934 noted "Some of the Shivaji's deeds, like the treacherous killing of the Bijapur general, lower him greatly in our estimation." Following a public outcry from Pune intellectuals, Congress leader T. R. Deogirikar noted that Nehru had admitted he was wrong regarding Shivaji, and now endorsed Shivaji as a great nationalist.

In 1966, the Shiv Sena (Army of Shivaji') political party was formed to promote the interests of Marathi speaking people in the face of migration to Maharashtra from other parts of India, and the accompanying loss of power for locals. His image adorns literature, propaganda and icons of the party.

In modern times, Shivaji is considered as a national hero in India, especially in the state of Maharashtra, where he remains an important figure in the state's history. Stories of his life form an integral part of the upbringing and identity of the Marathi people. Shivaji is upheld by regional political parties and also by the Maratha caste dominated Congress party's offshoots in Maharashtra, such as the Indira Congress and the Nationalist Congress Party.

In the late 20th century, Babasaheb Purandare became one of the most significant author in portraying Shivaji in his writings, leading him to be declared in 1964 as the Shiv-Shahir (lit. 'Bard of Shivaji'). However, Purandare, a Brahmin, was also accused of overemphasising the influence of Brahmin gurus on Shivaji, and his Maharashtra Bhushan award ceremony in 2015 was protested by those claiming he had defamed Shivaji.

In 1993, the Illustrated Weekly published an article suggesting that Shivaji was not opposed to Muslims per se, and that his style of governance was influenced by that of the Mughal Empire. Congress Party members called for legal actions against the publisher and writer, Marathi newspapers accused them of "imperial prejudice" and Shiv Sena called for the writer's public flogging. Maharashtra brought legal action against the publisher under regulations prohibiting enmity between religious and cultural groups, but a High Court found the Illustrated Weekly had operated within the bounds of freedom of expression.

In 2003, American academic James W. Laine published his book Shivaji: Hindu King in Islamic India to, what Ananya Vajpeyi terms, a regime of "cultural policing by militant Marathas". As a result of this publication, the Bhandarkar Oriental Research Institute in Pune where Laine had researched was attacked by the Sambhaji Brigade. Laine was even threatened to be arrested and the book was banned in Maharashtra in January 2004, but the ban was lifted by the Bombay High Court in 2007, and in July 2010 the Supreme Court of India upheld the lifting of the ban. This lifting was followed by public demonstrations against the author and the decision of the Supreme Court.

- **Statue of Shivaji opposite Gateway of India in South Mumbai**

Commemorations of Shivaji are found throughout India, most notably in Maharashtra. Shivaji's statues and monuments are found almost in every town and city in Maharashtra as well as in different places across India. Other commemorations include the Indian Navy's station INS Shivaji, numerous postage stamps, and the main airport and railway headquarters in Mumbai. In Maharashtra, there has been a long tradition of children building a replica fort with toy soldiers and other figures during the festival of Diwali in memory of Shivaji.

A proposal to build a giant memorial called Shiv Smarak was approved in 2016 to be located near Mumbai on a small island in the Arabian Sea. It will be 210 meters tall, making it the world's largest statue when completed in possibly 2021.

TWO

Chhatrapati Shivaji Birth Place Shivneri Fort

Shivneri Fort is a 17th-century military fortification located near Junnar in Pune district in Maharashtra, India. It is the birthplace of Chhatrapati Shivaji Maharaj, the emperor and founder of Maratha Empire.

Shivneri is known to be a place of Buddhist dominion from the 1st century AD. Its caves, rock-cut architecture and water system indicate the presence of habitation since 1st century AD. Shivneri got its name as it was under the possession of the Yadavas of Devagiri. This fort was mainly used to guard the old trading route from Desh to the port city of Kalyan. The place passed on to the Bahmani Sultanate after the weakening of Delhi Sultanate during the 15th century and it then passed on to the Ahmadnagar Sultanate in the 16th century.

In 1595, a Maratha chief named Maloji Bhonsle, the grandfather of Shivaji Bhosale, was enabled by the Ahmadnagar Sultan, Bahadur Nizam Shah and he gave him Shivneri and Chakan. Shivaji was born at the fort on 19 February 1630 (some accounts place it 1627), and spent his childhood there. Inside the fort is a small temple dedicated to goddess Shivai Devi, after whom Shivaji was named. The English traveller Fraze visited the fort in 1673 and found it invincible. According to his accounts, the fort was well-stocked to feed thousand families for seven years. The fort came under the control of the British Rule in 1820 after the Third Anglo-Maratha War.

- **Architecture Of Shivneri Fort**

Shivneri Fort is a hill fort having a triangular shape and has its entrance from the South-west side of the hill. Apart from the main gate there is an entrance to the fort from side called locally as the chain gate, where in one has to hold chains to climb up to the fort gate. The fort extends up to 1 mi (1.6 km) with seven spiral well-defended gates. There are mud walls all around the fort. Inside the fort, the major buildings are the prayer hall, a tomb and a mosque. There is an overhanging where executions took place. There are many gates structures protecting this fort. Mana Daravaja is one of the many gates of the fort. Its also called the origin of Tune.

At the centre of the fort is a water pond which is called 'Badami Talav', and to the south of this pond are statues of Jijabai and a young Shiva. In the fort there are two water springs, called Ganges and Yamuna, which have water throughout the year. Two kilometers away from this fort there are the Buddhist rock-cut caves, called Lenyadri caves, which is also one of Ashtavinayak temple in Maharashtra. It has been declared as a protected monument.The nearest town Junnar is a taluka place and is well connected by road. Junnar is about 90 km from Pune. The fort is at about 2–3 km from the junnar town. It is easy to reach the fort top via main entrance, however the trekkers with proper climbing equipment can try the chain route which is located on the western scarp of the fort. From the top of the fort, Narayangad, Hadsar, Chavand and Nimgiri forts can easily be seen.

THREE

ADIL SHAHI DYNASTY

The Adil Shahi or Adilshahi, was a Shia, and later Sunni Muslim, dynasty founded by Yusuf Adil Shah, that ruled the Sultanate of Bijapur, centred on present-day Bijapur district, Karnataka in India, in the Western area of the Deccan region of Southern India from 1489 to 1686. Bijapur had been a province of the Bahmani Sultanate (1347–1518), before its political decline in the last quarter of the 15th century and eventual break-up in 1518. The Bijapur Sultanate was absorbed into the Mughal Empire on 12 September 1686, after its conquest by the Emperor Aurangzcb.

The founder of the dynasty, Yusuf Adil Shah (1490–1510), was appointed Bahmani governor of the province, before creating a de facto independent Bijapur state. Yusuf and his son, Ismail, generally used the title Adil Khan. 'Khan', meaning 'Chief' in various Central Asian cultures and adopted in Persian, conferred a lower status than 'Shah', indicating royal rank. Only with the rule of Yusuf's grandson, Ibrahim Adil Shah I (1534–1558), did the title of Adil Shah come into common use. Even then, Bijapur rulers recognized Safavid Persian suzerainty over their realm.

The Bijapur Sultanate's borders changed considerably throughout its history. Its northern boundary remained relatively stable, straddling contemporary Southern Maharashtra and

Northern Karnataka. The Sultanate expanded southward, first with the conquest of the Raichur Doab following the defeat of the Vijayanagar empire at the Battle of Talikota in 1565. Later campaigns, notably during the reign of Mohammed Adil Shah (1627–1657), extended Bijapur's formal borders and nominal authority as far south as Bangalore. Bijapur was bounded on the West by the Portuguese state of Goa and on the East by the Sultanate of Golconda, ruled by the Qutb Shahi dynasty.

The former Bahmani provincial capital of Bijapur remained the capital of the Sultanate throughout its existence. After modest earlier developments, Ibrahim Adil Shah I (1534–1558) and Ali Adil Shah I (1558–1579) remodelled Bijapur, providing the citadel and city walls, congregational mosque, core royal palaces and major water supply infrastructure. Their successors, Ibrahim Adil Shah II (1580–1627), Mohammed Adil Shah (1627–1657) and Ali Adil Shah II (1657–1672), further adorned Bijapur with palaces, mosques, mausoleum and other structures, considered to be some of the finest examples of Deccan Sultanate and Indo-Islamic Architecture.

Bijapur was caught up in the instability and conflict resulting from the collapse of the Bahmani Empire. Constant warring, both with the Vijayanagar Empire and the other Deccan Sultanates, curtailed the development of state before the Deccan Sultanates allied to achieve victory over Vijayanagar at Talikota in 1565. Bijapur eventually conquered the neighbouring Sultanate of Bidar in 1619. The Portuguese Empire exerted pressure on the major Adil Shahi port of Goa, until it was conquered during the reign of Ibrahim II.

The Sultanate was thereafter relatively stable, although it was damaged by the revolt of Shivaji, whose father was Maratha commander in the service of Adil Shah. Shivaji founded an independent Maratha Kingdom which went on to become the Maratha Empire, one of the largest empires in India, just before the British conquered India. The greatest threat to Bijapur's security was, from the late 16th century, the expansion of the Mughal Empire into the Deccan. Although it may be the case that the Mughals destroyed the Adilshahi, it was Shivaji's revolt which weakened the

Adilshahi control. Various agreements and treaties imposed Mughal suzerainty on the Adil Shahs, by stages, until Bijapur's formal recognition of Mughal authority in 1636. The demands of their Mughal overlords sapped the Adil Shahs of their wealth until the Mughal conquest of Bijapur in 1686.

The founder of the dynasty, Yusuf Adil Shah, may have been a Georgian slave who was purchased by Mahmud Gawan from Iran. Yet, Salma Ahmed Farooqui, states, Yusuf was a son of the Ottoman Sultan Murad II. According to the historian Mir Rafi-uddin Ibrahim-i Shirazi, or Rafi', Yusuf's full name was Sultan Yusuf 'Adil Shah Savah or Sawah'i (from the ancient town of Saveh, southwest of modern Tehran), the son of Mahmud Beg of Sawa in Iran, (Rafi' 36–38, vide Devare 67, fn 2). Rafi's history of the 'Adil Shahi dynasty was written at the request of Ibrahim Adil Shah II, and was completed and presented to the patron in AH 1017. The Indian scholar T.N. Devare mentioned that while Rafi's account of the Bahmani dynasty is filled with anachronisms, his account of the Adilshahi is "fairly accurate, exhaustive, and possesses such rich and valuable information about Ali I and Ibrahim II" (312). Rafi-uddin later became the governor of Bijapur for about 15 years (Devare 316).

Yusuf's bravery and personality raised him rapidly in Sultan's favour, resulting in his appointment as the Governor of Bijapur. He built the Citadel or Arkilla and the Faroukh Mahal. Yusuf was a man of culture. He invited poets and artisans from Persia, Turkey, and Rome to his court. He's well known as a ruler who took advantage of the decline of the Bahmani power to establish himself as an independent sultan at Bijapur in 1498. He did this with a military support which has been given to him by a Bijapuri general Kalidas Madhu Sadhwani – brilliant commander and good diplomat, who made quick career by supporting Yusuf Adil Shah and then his son – Ismail Adil Shah. He married Punji, the sister of a Maratha Raja of Indapur. When Yusuf died in 1510, his son Ismail was still a boy. Punji in male attire valiantly defended him from a coup to grab the throne. Ismail Adil Shah thus became the ruler of Bijapur and succeeded his father's ambition.

- **Chand Bibi, the regent of Bijapur (1580–90)**

Ibrahim Adil Shah I who succeeded his father Ismail, fortified the city and built the old Jamia Masjid. Ali Adil Shah I who next ascended the throne, aligned his forces with other Muslim kings of Golconda, Ahmednagar and Bidar, and together, they brought down the Vijayanagar empire. With the loot gained, he launched ambitious projects. He built the Gagan Mahal, the Ali Rauza (his own tomb), Chand Bawdi (a large well) and the Jami Masjid. Ali I had no son, so his nephew Ibrahim II was set on the throne. Ali I's queen Chand Bibi had to aid him until he came of age. Ibrahim II was noted for his valor, intelligence and leanings towards the Hindu music and philosophy. Under his patronage the Bijapur school of painting reached its zenith. Muhammad Adil Shah succeeded his father Ibrahim II. He is renowned for Bijapur's grandest structure, the Gol Gumbaz, which has the biggest dome in the world with whispering gallery round about slightest sound is reproduced seven times. He also set up the historical Malik-e-Maidan, the massive gun.

Ali Adil Shah II inherited a troubled kingdom. He had to face the onslaught of the Maratha leader Shivaji on one side and Mughal emperor Aurangzeb on another. His mausoleum, Bara Kaman, planned to dwarf all others, was left unfinished due to his death. Sikandar Adil Shah, the last Adil Shahi sultan, ruled next for fourteen stormy years. Finally on 12 September 1686, the Mughal armies under Aurangzeb overpowered the city of Bijapur.

- **Sufis of Bijapur**

Arrival of Sufis in Bijapur region was started during the reign of Qutbuddin Aibak. During this period Deccan region was under the control of native Hindu rulers and Palegars. Shaikh Haji Roomi was the first to arrive in Bijapur with his companions. Although his other comrades like Shaikh Salahuddin, Shaikh Saiful Mulk and Syed Haji Makki were settled in Pune, Haidra and Tikota respectively.According to Tazkiraye Auliyae Dakkan i.e., Biographies of the saints of the Deccan, compiled by Abdul Jabbar Mulkapuri in 1912–1913,

Sufi Sarmast was one of the earliest sufi of this region. He came to the Deccan from Arabia in the 13th century at a time when the Deccan was a land of unbelievers with no sign of Islam or correct faith anywhere. His companions, pupils (fakir), disciples (murid), and soldiers (ghazi), numbered over seven hundred. He settled in Sagar in Sholapur district. There, a zealous and anti-Muslim raja named Kumaram (Kumara Rama) wished to expel Sufi Sarmast, and his companions having also prepared to a struggle, a bitter fight ensued. Heroes on both sides were slain. Finally the raja was killed by the hand of his daughter. Countless Hindus were killed, and at this time Lakhi Khan Afghan and Nimat Khan came from Delhi to assist him. Hindus were defeated and the Muslims were victorious. The rest of the Hindus, having accepted tributary status, made peace. Since by nature he was fundamentally not combative, Sufi Sarmast spread the religion of Mohammed and befriended the hearts of Hindus. Having seen his fine virtues and uncommon justice, many Hindus of that time accepted Islam, finally he died in the year A.H.680 i.e., 1281 A.D.

After this period arrival of Sufis in Bijapur and suburbs was started. Ainuddin Gahjul Ilm Dehelvi narrates that Ibrahim Sangane was one of the early Sufis of Bijapur parish. Sufis of Bijapur can be divided into three categories according to period of their arrival viz., Sufis before Bahmani and/or Adil Shahi Dynasty, Sufis during Adil Shahi Dynasty and Sufis after the fall of Adil Shahi Dynasty. And further, it can be classified as Sufis as warriors, Sufis as social reformers, Sufis as scholars, poets and writers.

Ibrahim Zubairi writes in his book Rouzatul Auliyae Beejapore (compiled during 1895) which describes that more than 30 tombs or Dargahs are there in Bijapur with more than 300 Khankahs i.e., Islamic Missionary Schools with notable number of disciples of different lineage like Hasani Sadat, Husaini Sadat, Razavi Sadat,

Kazmi Sadat, Shaikh Siddiquis, Farooquis, Usmanis, Alvis, Abbasees and other and spiritual chains like Quadari, Chishti, Suharwardi, Naqshbandi, Shuttari, Haidari etc.

- **In the second half**

In the second half of the 16th century, and the 17th century under the aegis of Adil Shahis, the capital city of Bijapur occupied a prominent place among the celebrated cities of India. It was a great centre of culture, trade and commerce, education and learning, etc. It was known for its own culture called, Bijapur Culture. During Bijapur's heyday of glory there was a conflux of different communities and the people. Sometimes in many respects it surpassed the great cities of Delhi and Agra of Mughal India. Before Yusuf Adil Shah, the founder of the Adil Shahis could make Bijapur as capital of his newly carved kingdom; the town occupied a considerable importance. The Khaljis made Bijapur their governor's seat, and after some time Khwajah Mahmud Gawan, the Bahmani premier constituted Bijapur region into a separate province. He owned property in Bijapur called "Kala Bagh".

He constructed a mausoleum of Ain-ud-Din Ganj-ul-'ullum. The architecture of the mausoleums of Zia-ud-Din Ghaznavi, Hafiz Husseini and Hamzah Husseini etc. suggests that these edifices belong to the Bahmani period. Thus Bijapur was fairly large town under the early Sultans of Adil Shahi dynasty. The capital progressed slowly, however, its star was in ascendancy since the accession of Sultan Ali Adil Shah I in 1558. His victory in the Battle of Talikota in 1565 and further campaigns in the Krishna-Tunghabhadra regions brought enormous wealth.

Hence he began to spend lavishly on its decoration. Under him every year saw some new building, a palace, a mosque, a bastion, or a minaret. His successor Ibrahim Adil Shah II added, so to say, a pearl necklace, Ibrahim Rouza to enhance the beauty of Bijapur, and Mohammed Adil Shah crowned it with a priceless gem called Gol Gumbaz. Thus the Adil Shahi monarchs poured their heart and soul in the capital city. The period between accessions of Ali Adil Shah I 1558 to the death of Mohammed Adil Shah 1656, can be called the golden age of the Adil Shahis as the kingdom flourished in all walks of life.

During the reign of Ibrahim Adil Shah II the population of Bijapur is stated to have reached 984,000 and had an incredible total of 1,600 mosques. Under Mohammed Adil Shah the population further increased. Historian J. D. B. Gribble writes.

in and around the suburbs of Shahpur only a million people lived. Within fort walls when shelter became difficult the Sultans founded the suburbs of Fatehpur, Aliabad, Shahpur or Khudanpur, Chandpur, Inayatpur, Ameenpur, Nawabpur, Latifpur, Fakirpur, Rasoolpur, Afzalpur, Padshahpur, Rambhapur, Aghapur (wrongly called Ogapur), Zohrapur, Khadijahpur, Habibpur, Salabatpur, Yarbipur, Tahwarpur, Sharzahpur, Yakubpur, Nauraspur, Dayanatpur, Sikandarpur, Quadirpur, Burhanpur, Khwaspur, Imampur, Ayinpur Bahamanhall, etc, these suburbs spread in circumference of fifteen miles of Bijapur. From all sides, the gates of Bijapur fort were thoroughly connected with roads, and the people had good amenities.

- **Adil Shahi Sultans made an Water system**

The Adil Shahi Sultans made an elaborate arrangement of pure and wholesome water for the people of Bijapur and its suburbs. At Torvi a masonry dam was constructed. We find another dam in its far eastern side. These two dams fed the reservoirs of Torvi and Afzalpur. Through these works, water was supplied to the suburbs of Shahpur, and the capital. Historian C. Schweitzer is of the opinion that the Torvi aqueduct is in itself a very credible engineering achievement of Adil Shahis.

To augment the existing water supply in the city Mohammed Adil Shah constructed Jahan Begum Lake (Begum Talab) in the south of Bijapur. This Lake fed the southern and eastern sides of the city. Thus water reached every comer of the capital. In addition, to supplement the water needs of the people in and around, the Sultans and nobles constructed big and small wells. Captain Sykes who visited Bijapur in 1819 reports, there were 700 wells (Boudis) with steps and 300 wells (Kuans or small wells) without steps within the walls of Bijapur. Moreover, we find the remains of tanks and lakes named Rangrez Talab, Quasim Talab, Fatehpur Talab and Allahpur Talab in the vicinity of Bijapur.

Begum Talab, which is 234.22-acre (0.9479 km2) tank was constructed in 1651 by Mohammad Adil Shah in memory of Jahan Begum. This tank was used for ensuring drinking water supply to the city. To the right side of lake there is an underground room from where water was supplied to city in earthen pipes. The pipes laid to depth of 15 feet (4.6 m) to 50 feet (15 m) were joined and cased in masonry. Many towers of height 25 feet (7.6 m) to 40 feet (12 m) called as "gunj" were built to release pressure of water and prevent pipes from bursting all along. These towers allowed dirt in pipes to remain at the bottom and clear water to flow.

- **Bazaars and Petes**

Bijapur being the capital and big business centre attracted merchants and travellers in large number from the Deccan and many parts of India and foreign lands. Abdal, a court poet in his Ibrahim Namah writes,(at the markets of Bijapur) the wealthy merchants of different countries sat in every direction (with their costly items).. In Bijapur the merchants could stay in the Sarais (inns) attached to the mosques or other public buildings. Such Sarais are found at Taj Boudi, Sandal Masjid, Bukhari Masjid, Ballad Khan Masjid etc. Nawab Mustafa Khan, a celebrated noble of Mohammed Adil Shah built a big Sarai in the west of Bijapur, which is now used as the District Jail.

From different parts of world many envoys, merchants, travellers, etc. visited Bijapur in its heyday of magnanimity and grandeur, and they left behind their valuable accounts of past grandiosities of Bijapur. In 1013 corresponding to (1604–1605) the

Mughal Emperor Akbar, commissioner Mirza Asad Baig, one of grandees of his court to Bijapur for diplomatic dealings. He was a person who saw Agra and Delhi in their glorious days. He wrote his account called, "Haalat-e-Asad Baig or Wakiat-e-Asad Baig". From his account we shall be able to form some idea of the position which Bijapur occupied among the wonder cities of India in the Medieval Ages. He cites in his impression of the city the grandeurs of the Adil Shahi court and its customs:

On 17th of Shaaban I marched forward with attendants that were with me to meet Adil Khan (Ibrahim Adil Shah II), and was introduced to him in a building upon that lake Gagan Mahal at Bijapur appointed for such ceremonies. It was a very pleasant spot appropriately furnished. In two or three houses the rooms were in a perfect tip-top condition, and after prayer on that day Adil Khan came, wish all pomp and circumstances, followed by a retinue of elephants... that palace, which they called "Hajjah" All around the gate of my residence were lofty buildings with houses and porticoes; the situation was very healthy and airy. It lies in open space in the city. Its northern portico is to the east of a "Bazaar" of a great extent, as much as thirty yards wide and about two Kos long. Before each shop was a beautiful green tree, and the whole "Bazaar" was extremely clean and pure.

It was filled with rare goods, such as are not seen or heard of in any other town. There were shops of cloths sellers, jewellers, armourers, vintners, fish-mongers, and cooks... in the jeweller's shops were jewels of all sorts, wrought into variety. of articles, such as daggers, knives, mirrors, necklaces, and "laso" into the form of birds, such as parrots, doves and peacocks, etc. all studded with valuable jewels, and arranged upon shelves, rising one above the other. By the side of this shop will be a baker's with rare viands, placed in the same manner, upon tiers of shelves in like manner.

Then a clothier's, then a spirit merchant's with various sorts of China vessels, valuable crystal bottles, costly cups, filled with choice and rare essence, arrayed on shelves, while in the front of the shop were jars of double-distilled spirits. Besides that shop will be a fruiter's, filled with all kinds of fruits and sweetmeats, such as pistachios nuts, and relishes, and sugar-candy and almonds. On another side may be a wine merchant's shop, and an establishment of singers, dancers and beautiful women adorned with various kinds of jewels, and fair-faced choristers, all ready to perform whatever may be desired of them. In short, the whole "Bazaar" was filled with wine and beauty, dances, perfumes, jewels, of all sorts, plates, and viands.

In one street were a thousand bands of people drinking, and dancers, lovers, and pleasure-seekers assembled; none quarrelled or disputed with one another and this state of things was perpetual. Perhaps no place in the wide world could present a more wonderful spectacle to the eye of the traveller... (for Emperor Akbar) I purchased for Rs. 25900 emeralds, "pokhraj", "Nilam" and birds made of jewels. I purchased the diamond and "Dugdugi" for Rs. 55000 and agreed to pay the price after Mir Jamaluddin approves.

Mirza Asad Baig left Bijapur on 24 January 1604. His graphic account of Bijapur tells us how this city was prosperous, rich and flourishing. Another traveller Manctelslo, who visited the Deccan area in 1638 writes,

Bijapur was one of the greatest cities in the whole of Asia, more than five "leagues" (i.e., fifteen miles) the city had five great suburbs where most of the traders lived and in Scyanpur (Shahpur) were most of the jewelers dealing in costly pearls.

Similarly, Jean Baptiste Tavernier, who visited India between 1631 and 1667, was a jeweller, probably he had been to Bijapur for selling some of his jewels. He has left for us an account, in which he describes Bijapur was a great city ... in its large suburbs many goldsmiths and jewellers dwelt ... the king's palace (Arkillah or citadel) was vast, but ill-built and the access to it was very dangerous as the ditch with which it was girt was full of crocodiles,. in the same way, the Dutch traveller, Baldeous, the English geographer, Ogilby and others praise the greatness of Bijapur.

The Adil Shahi Sultans were fond of gardens, water pavilions and resorts; hence they beautified Bijapur by presence of such amusing spots. Rafiuddin Shirazi writes in his “"Tazkiratul-Mulk"” that during the rule of Ibrahim Adil Shah I a garden 60 yards long and 60 yards broad, was laid within the outer “Hissar” (i.e., Arbah) and another 20 yards long and 20 yards broad, within the inner one (i.e., Arkilla Wall or citadel) was constructed. In the reign of Ali Adil Shah I, many trees of fruits viz. odoriferous orange, date, grapes, pomegranate, figs, apple. “Naar” (quince-like fruit), etc. brought from the countries of hot and cold climates were set in gardens.

From different historical sources we get references of gardens like Kishwar Khan Bagh, Ali Bagh, Dou-az-Deh (twelve) Imam Bagh, Alavi Bagh, Arkillah Bagh, Nauroz Bagh, Ibrahim Bagh, Murari Bagh, Naginah Bagh, etc. in Bijapur. In southern side in the capital, a renowned Adil Shahi noble, Mubarak Khan constructed water pavilions and resort. Likewise, at Kumatagi village, about 12 miles in the east of Bijapur, the Sultans laid the water pavilions and resort for royal members.

Before the Muslims could establish their rule in Bijapur, it was a great centre of learning in South India. It is evident from the bilingual Marathi–Sanskrit inscription, which is inscribed just under the Persian epigraph in the Karimuddin mosque 16 that the city of Bijapur is given the title of “"Banaras of the South"”. Since ancient time Banaras in northern India was a celebrated centre of learning.

The Khaiji governor of Bijapur, Malik Karimuddin, probably found at this place the great activities of learning; hence he entitled Bijapur as the Banaras of the South. The Khaljis conquered whole south India and they were well acquainted with its famous cities like Daulatabad of Yadavas, Warangal of Kakatiyas, Dwarasamudra of Hoysalas and Madurai of Pandyas. However, they did not entitle any of these cities as the Banaras of the South, except Bijapur, though these cities were the capitals of ruling dynasties. During the rule of Bahmanis Bijapur retained its academic excellence. The renowned learned Sufi of India, Ainuddin Ganjuloom Junnaidi, who authored 125 works of Qur’anic commentaries, Quirat (art of Quranic recitation), Hadith (prophetic Traditions), Scholasticism,

Principles of Law, Fique (Islamic Law), Suluk (behavior). Syntax, Lexicography, Ansaab (genealogy). History, Tibb (medicine), Hilmat, Sanf (grammaIj), Quasidah, etc. lived in from 1371, until his death in 1390.

His disciple and other Sufis like Ibrahim Sangani and his sons, Abdullah AI-Ghazani, Ziauddin Ghazanavi and Shah Hamzah Hussaini kept their noble litterateur's traditions alive in Bijapur. Under the aegis of Adil Shahis of Bijapur advanced very much in the field of learning. It was considered as the 'Second Baghdad' in scholastic activities in the Islamic world. Owing to its popularity in this sphere Ibrahim Adil Shah II named it ""Vidhyapur" All Sultans of Bijapur were men of letters. Ali Adil Shah I was well versed in religion, logic, sciences, syntax, etymology and grammar. He was fond of reading to the extent that he kept with him big boxes of books, while on tour. All Sultans patronised the teachers and scholars. It was routine in the capital that the scholars met at different places, and among them learned discussions were held.

At the capital the Royal Library existed in which nearly sixty men, calligraphers, gilders of books, book binders and illuminators were busy doing their work whole day in the library. Sesh Waman Pandit was the Royal Librarian. Ibrahim-II's court poet Baqir Khurd-e-Kasm worked as transcriber in the Royal Library. The noted scholars in the capital were Shah Nawaz Khan, Abdul Rasheed-al-Bastagi, Shah Sibagatullah Hussaini, Shaikh Alimullah Muhaddis (a teacher of Sayings or Traditions of Muhummad, and Theology in Jumma mosque), Mullan Hassan Faraghi, MullanHabibullah, Shah Mohummad Mulki and Shah Habibullah Hussaini. Shah Zayn Muqbil, a great lover of learning and books, had eight hundred manuscripts in his library, out of these over three hundred were written by him. Miran Mohummad Mudarris Hussaini was also a great teacher.

At the Asar Mahal there were two Madrasas (religious schools), one for teaching Hadith (Tradition) and another for Fiqah and Imaan (Theology and Belief). Free education with delicious food, and stipend of one Hun to each student was provided. The Mosques had the Maktabs (elementary schools) where Arabic and Persian studies were taught. The state supplied books free of costs. The students who performed excellently in the annual examination, received prizes in Huns, and later appointed in high and honourable position. Besides these, most of the Sufis maintained their own Khankhas (convents for disciples) and Kutub Khanas (libraries). Even to this day some of the descendants of Sufis in perpetuity continued this tradition.

In consequence of state patronage, a bulk of literature in Arabic, Persian and Dakhani Urdu had come up. In addition, the languages like Sanskrit, Marathi and Kannada flourished. Pandit Narhari, a court poet of Ibrahim Adil Shah II, composed the poetic excellence on his master, called, Nauras Manzarf. Shri Laxmipathi, a disciple of Pandit Rukmangada composed a number of Marathi and Hindi devotional songs set in musical Ragas. Swamy Yadvendra was also a prominent contributor in Marathi literature. In the south of kingdom, the official transaction was carried out in Kannada.

- **The Bahmani Kingdom, Kandesh, and the Five Sultanates**

Dr. Zaman Khodaey says, in the kingdom of Bijapur the medical aids and Darush-Shafa existed. In the hospitals the different Departments dealt and treated different fevers, eye and ear problems, skin and other diseases. We have references that in the kingdom the physicians practised the Unani, Ayurvedic, Irani and European systems of medicine. Hakim Gilani and Farnalope Firangi, a European physician and surgeon worked under Ibrahim Adil Shah II. Farnalope treated his ailing patron wrongly, which caused Sultan's death. Khawas Khan caught him, and as a punishment his nose and lips were cut off.

Nothing daunted, Fanalope returned to his home and cut off the nose and lips of one of his slaves, and so fastened the same to his own that he was soon cured even of scars. He lived long in Bijapur and resumed his practice with great success. Aithippa, an Ayurvedic physician, who was attached to a dispensary at Bijapur compiled for his son Champa, Tibb-e-Bahri-o-Barri, a treatise on medicine. It contains a short vocabulary of some parts of the human body and some drugs with their equivalent in Arabic and Urdu. It further contains hints as to the examination of patients and symptoms and treatment of diseases. He had spent a long time attending upon and getting instruction from Hakim Mohummad Hussain Unani and Hakim Mohammad Masum Isfahani.

The great historian Firishta was an expert Ayurvedic physician. He studied this system under Hakim-e-Misri and other Hindu physicians. After attaining proficiency, he started his own dispensary and prepared patent drugs and popular medicines. He possessed a great knowledge of Sanskrit, hence studied thoroughly works of Ayurveda like the Samhitas of Wagbhat, Charak and Sushrut, and wrote Dastur-e- Attibba or Iktiyarat-e-Qasmi. In this book, he mentioned the names of famous Ayurvedic physicians like Jagdeva, Sagarbhat and Sawa Pandit. He cites in the names of various diseases, herbs and drugs and also discusses simple and compound medicines and formulae of their preparation. The book is fairly comprehensive as its scope extends to anatomy, physiology and therapy. It seems Firishta was an expert in Botany as well. He gave details of minutes regarding characteristics of medicinal herbs, plants and fruits of India.

Another physician Hakim Rukna-e-Maish skilled in medicine stayed in the court of Ibrahim Adil Shah II for some time before he joined the Mughals. At the instance of the same Sultan; Yunus Beg completed Kitab-e-TIbb, a work on medicine. The court poet of Mohammed Adil Shah, Hakim Aatishi possessed a unique skill in medicine and served as the Royal Physician. He was a personal physician of the Sultan, without his permission he could not attend other patients. With permission once he cured Khan-e-Khanan Ikhlas Khan. Aatishi took this onerous duty only when other physicians altogether failed. By his miraculous treatment patients recovered within three weeks. Thus the Adil Shahi Sultans and the nobles never overlooked the medical services and always encouraged the physicians giving them handsome rewards. It because of such encouragement some of the physicians produced literature on medicine.

The Adil Shahi monarchs were great lovers of music; some of them attained high order. Yusuf Adil Shah played "Tambur"(Tambourine) and "Ud" (lute). Ismail Adil Shah had high admiration for Central Asian music. Music received greater encouragement under Ibrahim Adil Shah II. He was the greatest musician of his age. He was poet and singer and maintained an inordinately a large number of musicians and minstrels (three or four thousand) at his court.

The band of musicians was known as Lashkar-e-Nauras (army of Nauras) they were paid by the government regularly. At Nauraspur he constructed Sangeet Mahal and residential mansions for songsters, minstrels and dancing girls. With great pomp the festival of Nauras (musical concert) was celebrated during his time. In a number of paintings Ibrahim Adil Shah II was depicted playing musical instruments like "Tambur", "Sitar", "Veena" and "Guitar". Emperor Jahangir, and Mirza Asad Baig the Mughal envoy considerably praised Ibrahim Adil Shah II's love for music. Mirza Asad Baig writes in his "Wakiyat" that he was invited to the royal palace to bid farewell to Ibrahim Adil Shah II.

A grand show of music had been arranged for this occasion. He found the Sultan so wrapped up in listening to the music that he could hardly reply to Asad Baig's questions. The conversation between them for some time mainly concerned music and musicians. The Sultan wanted to know whether Emperor Akbar was fond of music and Asad Baig informed him that the Emperor did sometime listen to music. The Sultan then wanted to know whether Tansen stood or sat while singing before the Emperor and was told that in the Darbar or during day time Tansen had to stand while singing, but at night and on the occasion of Nauroz and Jashan festival Tansen and other musicians were permitted to sit while singing. The Sultan told Asad Baig, "Music is such that it should be heard at all times and always, and musicians should be kept happy.

- **Art and architecture**

The Adil Shahi Sultans had concentrated their energies almost exclusively on architecture and the allied arts, each Sultan endeavouring to excel his predecessor in the number, size, or splendor of his building projects. The architecture of Bijapur is a combination of Persian, Ottoman Turkish and Deccani styles. It is amazing to note mat in Ibrahim Rouzah, Dilkusha Mahal (Mahatar Mahal), Malikah-e-Jahan Mosque, Jal Mahal, etc. the Bijapur sculptors have carved beautiful designs in stones, as the carpenters do in wood. The stucco plaster designing in some monuments is superb.

- **Adil Shahi arts and heritage**

A manuscript depicting the ruler of Bijapur in the year 1591, Ibrahim Adil Shah II.The contribution of the Adil Shahi kings to the architecture, painting, language, literature and music of Karnataka is unique. Bijapur (Kannada form of the Sanskrit Vidyapur or Vidyanagari) became a cosmopolitan city, and it attracted many scholars, artists, musicians, and Sufi saints from Turkey, Persia (Iran) Iraq, Turkey, Turkestan, etc.

The unfinished Jami Masjid, started in 1565, has an arcaded prayer hall with fine aisles supported on massive piers has an impressive dome. The Ibrahim Rouza which contains the tomb of Ibrahim Adil Shah II, is a fine structure with delicate carvings. Persian artists of Adil Shahi court have left a rare treasure of miniature paintings, some of which are well-preserved in Europe's great museums.

The Dakhani language, an amalgam of Persian-Arabic, Urdu, Marathi, and Kannada, developed into an independent spoken and literary language. Under the Adil Shahis many literary works were published in Dakhani. Ibrahim Adil Shah II's book of poems and music, Kitab-e-Navras is in Dakhani. The Mushaira (poetic symposium) was born in the Bijapur court and later travelled north.

The Dakhani language, which was growing under the Bahamani kings, later came to be known as Dakhan Urdu to distinguish it from the North Indian Urdu. Adil Shah II played the sitar and ud and Ismail was a composer.

- **Asar Mahal**

Muhammad Qasim Firishta wrote that in the year AH 1008, Mir Mohammed Swaleh Hamadani came to Bijapur. He had with him hair of the Muhammad ("Mooy-e-Mubarrak"). Sultan Ibrahim Adil shah heard of this and rejoiced. Met Mir Swaleh Hamdani, the King saw the hair and gave priceless gifts to Mir Sahab. Mir Sahab gave two strands of the hair to Sultan Ibrahim Adil Shah. At first, they were kept in Gagan Mahal, but during the reign of Adil Shah a huge fire burned down Gagan Mahal.

Everything there burnt up, except the two boxes in which two strands of hair were kept. In the midst of the conflagration, a Sufi Saint named Syed Saheb Mohiuddin braved the flames, entered and carried the boxes out on his head; the Sultan then kept these boxes in Asar Mahal. The custody of "Mooy-e-Mubarrak" has been given to the saint Noor Muhammad Mushraff issued by AdliShahi Diwan. Till today, the Original Sanad is with Mushrif family. Annual function is celebrated every year on 12th Rabi-ul-awwal (Sandal & Urs Asar Mahal). This function is held regularly since from more than 350 years.

It is said that in the year AH 1142 Adil Shah used to frequently view these strands of hair. On one occasion he asked all the Sufis of that time to come and see them. So Hashim Husaini and Sayyad Shah Murtuza Quadri came there and asked to open the boxes; they were opened in front of the noble persons. But as they were opened a bright ray was everywhere. Nobody could bear the brightness of the ray and they all became unconscious. Everywhere there was a perfume and then everybody saw the hair. After that period it is said that the boxes were neither opened nor had a privilege.

FOUR

BHONSLE DYNASTY

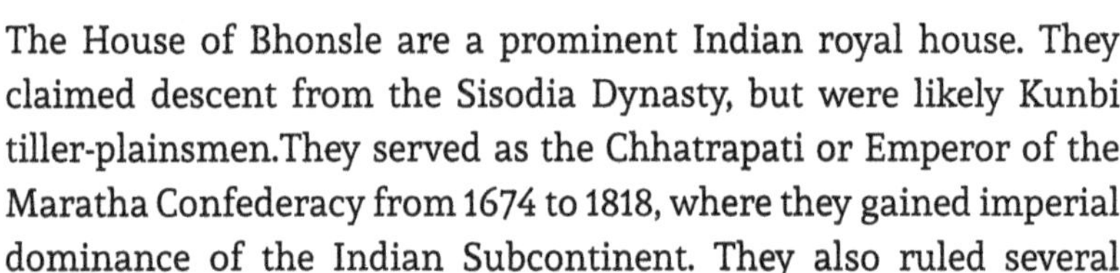

The House of Bhonsle are a prominent Indian royal house. They claimed descent from the Sisodia Dynasty, but were likely Kunbi tiller-plainsmen.They served as the Chhatrapati or Emperor of the Maratha Confederacy from 1674 to 1818, where they gained imperial dominance of the Indian Subcontinent. They also ruled several states such as Satara, Kolhapur, Thanjavur, Nagpur, Akkalkot, Sawantwadi and Barshi.

The House of Bhonsle was founded in 1577 by Maloji Bhosale, a predominant general or sardar of Malik Ambar of the Ahmadnagar Sultanate. In 1595 or 1599, Maloji was given the title of raja by Bahadur Nizam Shah, the ruler of the Ahmadnagar Sultanate. He was later granted was given the jagir of Pune, Elur (Verul), Derhadi, Kannarad and Supe. He was also given control over the first of the Shivneri and Chakan. These positions were inherited by his sons Shahaji and Sharifji, who were named after a Muslim Sufi Shah Sharif

The origins of the Bhonsles in unclear. According to Jadunath Sarkar and other scholars, Bhonsles were predominantly Deccani tiller-plainsmen from the Shudra caste; they were part of the Marathas/Kunbis, an amorphous class-group. Scholars have however disagreed about the agricultural status of Bhosles. Rosalind O'Hanlon notes that the historical evolution of castes grouped under the Maratha-Kunbis is sketchy. Ananya Vajpeyi rejects the designation of Shudra, since the category has remained in a state of flux across centuries; she instead notes them to be a Marathi lineage, who enjoyed "reasonably high" social status as landholders and warlords, being in the service of Deccan Sultanate or Mughals.

According to R. C. Dhere's interpretation of local oral history and ethnography, Bhonsles descend from the Hoysalas and Yadavas of Devagiri, who were cow-herding Gavli sovereigns. In early thirteenth century, "Baliyeppa Gopati Sirsat", a Hoysala cousin of Simhana migrated from Gadag to Satara along with his pastoral herd and kul-devta; the Sambhu Mahadev was thus installed at a hill-top in Singhnapur. Historical records indicate that this shrine received extensive patronage from Maloji onwards. Further, there exists a branch of the Bhosles named "Sirsat Bhosles" and Bhosle (or "Bhosale") is linguistically similar to "Hoysala". M. K. Dhavalikar found the work to convincingly explain the foundation of the Bhosle clan (as well as Sambhu Mahadev cult). Vajpeyi too advocates that Dhere's theory be probed in greater detail — "rom pastoralist big men to warlords on horseback, is not an impossible distance to cover in two to three centuries."

- **Shivaji's In 1670**

By 1670s, Shivaji had acquired extensive territory and wealth from his campaigns. But, lacking a formal crown, he had no operational legitimacy to rule his de facto domain and technically, remained subject to his Mughal (or Deccan Sultanate) overlords; in the hierarchy of power, Shivaji's position remained similar to fellow Maratha chieftains. Also, he was often opposed by the orthodox Brahmin community of Maharashtra. A coronation sanctioned by the Brahmins was thus planned, in a bid to proclaim sovereignty and legitimize his rule.

On proposing the Brahmins of his court to have him proclaimed as the rightful king, a controversy erupted: the regnal status was reserved for those belonging to the kshatriya varna. Not only was there a fundamental dispute among scholars on whether any true

Kshatriya survived in the Kali Yuga, having been all destroyed by Parashurama but also Shivaji's grandfather was a tiller-headman, Shivaji did not wear the sacred thread, and his marriage was not in accordance with the Kshatriya customs. Thus, the Brahmins had him categorised as a shudra.

Compelled to postpone his coronation, Shivaji had his secretary Balaji Avji Chitnis sent to the Sisodiyas of Mewar for inspection of the royal genealogies; Avji returned with a favorable finding — Shahji turned out to be a descendant of Chacho Sisodiya, a half-Rajput uncle of Mokal Singh. Gaga Bhatt, a famed Brahmin of Banaras, was then hired to ratify Chitnis' find, and the Bhonsles were now permitted to stake a claim to Kshatriya caste. The coronation would be re-executed in June 1674 but only after going through a long list of preludes.

Led by Bhatt, who employed traditional Hindu imagery in an unprecedented scale, the first phase had Shivaji penance for having lived as a Maratha despite being a Kshatriya. Then came the sacred thread ceremony ('maunjibandhanam') followed by remarriage according to Kshatriya customs ('mantra-vivah') and a sequence of Vedic rituals before the eventual coronation ('abhisheka') — a public spectacle of enormous expense that heralded the rebirth of Shivaji as a Kshatriya king. Panegyrics composed by court-poets during these spans (and afterward) reinforced onto the public memory that Shivaji (and the Bhonsles) indeed belonged from the Sisodiyas.

However, the Kshatriyization was not unanimous; a section of Brahmins continued to deny the Kshatriya status. Brahmins of the Peshwa period rejected Bhatt's acceptance of Shivaji's claims and blamed the non-dharmic coronation for all ills that plagued Shivaji and his heirs—in tune with the general Brahminical sentiment to categorize all Marathas as Shudras, carte-blanche; there have been even claims that Bhatt was excommunicated by Maratha Brahmins for his role in the coronation of Shivaji Interestingly, all claims to Rajput ancestry had largely vanished from the family's subsequent projections of identity.

Vajpeyi notes the "veridical status" of Chitnis' finds to be not determinable to "historical certainty" — the links were tenuous at best and inventive at worst. Shivaji was not a Rajput and the sole purpose of the lineage was to guarantee Shivaji's consecration as a Kshatriya, in a tactic that had clear parallels to Rajputisation. Jadunath Sarkar deemed that the genealogy was cleverly fabricated by Balaji Awji and after some reluctance accepted by Gaga Bhatt, who in turn was "rewarded with a huge fee". V. K. Rajwade, Dhere, Allison Busch, John Keay and Audrey Truschke also agree with Sarkar about the fabrication. G. S. Sardesai notes that the descent is "not authentically proved". Stewart N. Gordon does not pass any judgement but notes Bhatt to be a "creative Brahmin". André Wink deems that the Sisodia genealogical claim is destined to remain disputed forever.

- **Ahmadnagar Sultanate**

The earliest accepted members of the Bhonsles are Mudhoji Bhonsle and his kin Rupaji Bhonsle, who were the village headman (pāṭīl) of Hingani — this branch has been since known as Hinganikar Bhonsles. A branch seem to have split soon, who went on to claim an ancestral right to the post of district steward (deśmukhī) of Kadewalit: Suryaji Bhonsle during the reign of Ahmad Nizam Shah I (early 1490s), and his son Sharafji Bhonsle during the conquest of the region by Daniyal Mirza (1599). This branch has been since known as Kadewalit Bhonsles.

The next significant Bhonsle was probably Maloji Bhosale from the Hinganikar branch. He was the great-grandson of one Kheloji (c. 1490).The House of Bhonsle was offically founded by Maloji Bhosale who initially served as a patil (chief) of the Hingni Berdi and Devalgaon villages around Pune. Later, along with his brother Vithoji, he migrated to Sindkhed and served as a Horseman.

In 1577, they joined the service of the Ahmadnagar Sultanate, under Sultan Murtaza Nizam Shah I. Maloji became a trusted General of the Peshwa Malik Amber fighting against rival powers such as the Mughals and Bijapur Sultanate the parganas (administrative units) of Elur (Verul), Derhadi and Kannarad. In 1595 or 1599, Maloji was given the title of raja by Bahadur Nizam Shah, officially establishing the House of Bhonsle. On the recommendation of Malik Ambar, he was given the jagir of Pune and Supe parganas, along with the control of the Shivneri and Chakan forts. Maloji carried out the restoration of the Grishneshwar temple near Verul, and also constructed a large tank at the Shambhu Mahadev temple in Shikhar Shingnapur. Maloji and his wife Uma Bai had 2 sons: Shahaji and Sharifji, named Sufi Pir Hazrat Shah Sharif.

According to Shivabharata, composed by Shivaji's court poet Paramananda, Maloji's wife Umabai prayed to the Sufi Pir Shah Sharif of Ahmadnagar to bless her with a son. She gave birth to two sons, who were named Shahaji and Sharifji after the Pir.

- **Mughal–Maratha Wars**

The Maratha Empire was established by Shivaji I the grandson of Maloji in 1674. This was established to invasions from the Mughal Empire and the Bijapur Sultanate. Shivaji's forces initially occupied the Fort of Torna in 1642. He had expanded his kingdom to Raigad by 1674. he crowned himself He was crowned as Chhatrapati, meaning emperor.Shivaji wanted to establish his government based on his Philosophy of Hindavi Swarajya. (The Rule of the People) This advocated for more representation of the people and less power of the elites. He later established the Ashta Pradhan, (Modern council of ministers) an institution of a council of eight ministers to guide the administration of his nascent state. Each of the ministers was placed in charge of an administrative department; thus, the council heralded the birth of a bureaucracy. Shivaji appointed Moropant Trimbak Pingle as the Peshwa, the leader of the council.

Shivaji was succeeded by his son Sambhaji I. In early 1689, Sambhaji and his commanders met at Sangameshwar. Mughal forces, under Emperor Aurangzeb attacked Sangameshwar when

Sambhaji was accompanied by just a few men. Sambhaji captured by the Mughal troops on 1 February 1689. Aurangzeb had charged Sambhaji with attacks by Maratha forces on Burhanpur. He and his advisor, Kavi Kalash, were taken to Bahadurgad by the imperial army, where they were executed by the Mughals on 21 March 1689.

After the execution of Sambhaji, Rajaram I was crowned at Raigad on 12 March 1689. During the Mughal started siege on Raigad on 25 March 1689, the widow of Sambhaji (Maharani Yesubai) and Peshwa Ramchandra Pant Amatya sent young Rajaram to the stronghold of Pratapgad through Kavlya ghat. Rajaram to escape through Kavlya ghat to the fort of Jinji through the Pratapgad and Vishalgad forts, Rajaram reached Keladi in disguise and pursued assistance from Keladi Chennamma - who kept the Mughal attack in check to ensure safe passage and escape of Rajaram to Jinji where he reached after a month and a half on 1 November 1689.Aurangzeb sent Uzbek general Ghazi-ud-din Firoze Jung against the Marathas in the Deccan. He then sent Zulfiqar Khan Nusrat Jung to capture the Jingi Fort. He laid siege to it in September, 1690. After three failed attempts, it was finally captured after seven years on 8 January 1698. Rajaram, however, escaped and fled first to Vellore and later to Vishalgad. Rajaram returned to jinji and occupied the fort 11 November 1689, but left before it fell in 1698, setting up his court at fort Satara. Then, Maratha commanders, Santaji Ghorpade and Dhanaji Jadhav, defeated the Mughal forces, therefore cutting off their lines of communication in Jingi.

***hindi trans remaing kolhapur

- **Kolhapur State**

In 1707, Mughal Emperor Muhammad Azam Shah released Shahu Bhosale, the son of Sambhaji. However, his mother was kept as a hostage of the Mughals, in order to ensure that Shahu adhered to the release conditions. Immediately the Maratha throne was claimed his aunt Tarabai, claiming the throne for her son Shivaji II. After his victory at the Battle of Khed, Shahu established himself at

Satara, forcing her to retire with her son to Kolhapur. This resulted in the creation of the Kolhapur branch in 1709 under Tarabai, splitting from the main Satara branch under Shahu.. Shivaji II and Tarabai were soon deposed by Rajasbai, the other widow of Rajaram. She installed her own son, Sambhaji II as the new ruler of Kolhapur. Sambhaji then made alliance with the Nizam. The defeat of the Nizam by Bajirao I in the Battle of Palkhed in 1728 led to the former ending his support for Sambhaji. Sambhaji II signed the Treaty of Warna in 1731 with his cousin Shahuji to formalize the two separate seats of Bhonsle family.

- **Maratha Empire**

Shahu appointed Balaji Vishwanath a member of the Bhat Family as his Peshwa. The Peshwa was instrumental in securing Mughal recognition of Shahu as the rightful heir of Shivaji and the Chhatrapati of the Marathas. Balaji also gained the release of Shahu's mother, Yesubai, from Mughal captivity in 1719.

The Peshwas later became de facto rulers of the Maratha Empire. Under the Peshwas, Chhatrapati was limited to simply a monarchial figurehead. Maratha Empire dominated most of the Indian subcontinent.Under the Peshwas the Marathas expanded to their greatest extent. 1737, Under Bajirao I invaded Delhi in a blitzkrieg manner at the Battle of Delhi (1737). The Nizam set out from the Deccan to rescue the Mughals from the invasion of the Marathas, but was defeated decisively in the Battle of Bhopal. The Marathas extracted a large tribute from the Mughals and signed a treaty which ceded Malwa to the Marathas. The Battle of Vasai was fought between the Marathas and the Portuguese in Vasai, a village lying on the northern shore of Vasai creek. (Part of modern day Mumbai)

After Shahu's death, he was succeeded by Rajaram II When Peshwa Balaji Baji Rao left for the Mughal frontier, Tarabai urged Rajaram II to remove him from the post of Peshwa. When Rajaram refused, she imprisoned him in a dungeon at Satara, on 24 November 1750. She claimed that he was an imposter from

Gondhali caste and she had falsely presented him as her grandson to Shahu. His health deteriorated considerably during this imprisonment. On 14 September 1752, Tarabai and Balaji Rao took an oath at Khandoba temple in Jejuri, promising mutual peace. Nevertheless, the Peshwa retained Rajaram II as the titular Chhatrapati and a powerless figurehead.Peshwa Bajirao and his three chiefs, Pawar (Dhar), Holkar (Indore), and Scindia (Gwalior), expanded it northwards up to Peshawar. He also expanded it up to Kaveri river.

- **Bhonsles of Nagpur**

After the death of Chand Sultan, the Gond ruler of Deogarh, in 1739, there were quarrels over the succession, leading to the throne being usurped by Wali Shah, an illegitimate son of Bakht Buland Shah. Chand Sultan's widow Ratan Kunwar invoked the aid of the Maratha leader Raghoji Bhonsle of Berar in the interest of her sons Akbar Shah and Burhan Shah. Wali Shah was put to death and the rightful heirs placed on the throne. Raghoji I Bhonsle was sent back to Berar with a plentiful bounty for his aid. Raghoji then declared himself the King of Nagpur and the 'protector' of the Gond king. Thus in 1743, Burhan Shah was practically made a state pensionary, with real power being in the hands of the Maratha ruler. After this event the history of the Gond kingdom of Deogarh is not recorded.

During Shahu's reign, Raghoji Bhosale of Nagpur expanded the empire Eastwards, reaching present-day Bengal. Khanderao Dabhade and later his son, Triambakrao, expanded it Westwards into Gujarat. In the Battle of Damalcherry in 1740, which was a major confrontation with the Nawab of the Carnatic, Dost Ali Khan . Raghoji was victorious and increased Maratha Influence in the Carnatic.

after the successful campaign in Carnatic at the Battle of Trichinopolly. Raghoji invaded Bengal. Raghoji was able to annex Orissa and parts of Bengal permanently as he successfully exploited the chaotic conditions prevailing in the region after the death of their Governor Murshid Quli Khan in 1727.Nawab of Bengal ceded territory up to the river Suvarnarekha to the Marathas, and agreeing to pay Rs. 20 lacs as chauth for Bengal (includes both West Bengal and Bangladesh) and 12 lacs for Bihar (including Jharkhand), thus Bengal becoming a tributary to the Marathas.

the Kingdom of Nagpur at its greatest extent in 1751.After Raghoji's death, he was succeeded by his son Janoji Bhonsle. Janoji was involved in wars between the Peshwa and the Nizam of Hyderabad. The nizam united against him and sacked and burnt Nagpur in 1765. On Janoji's death on 21 May 1772, the Battle of Panchgaon was fought over succession, until Mudhoji Bhonsle was victorious. In 1785 Mandla and the upper Narmada valley were added to the Nagpur dominions by treaty with the Peshwa. Mudhoji also had close ties with the British East India Company. Mudhoji was succeeded by Raghoji II. he who acquired Hoshangabad and the lower Narmada valley.

In 1803 he united with Daulat Rao Sindhia of Gwalior against the British, and their alliance with Nizam Ali Khan of Hyderabad. The British and the Nizam were victorias at the battles of Assaye and Argaon, and signed the Treaty of Deogaon of that year Raghoji ceded Cuttack, southern Berar, and Sambalpur to the British, although Sambalpur was reconquered by 1806 by Raghoji. Raghoji II was deprived of a third of his territories, and he attempted to make up the loss of revenue from the remainder. The villages were mercilessly rack-rented, and many new taxes imposed. At the same time the raids of the Pindaris commenced. In 1811 they advanced to Nagpur and burnt the suburbs. Raghoji rebuilt many of the damaged village and forts. On the death of Raghoji II in 1816, his son Parsoji was supplanted and murdered by Mudhoji II Bhonsle, In 1817.

A treaty of alliance providing for the maintenance of a subsidiary force by the British was signed in this year, a British resident having been appointed to the Nagpur court since 1799. In 1817, on the outbreak of war between the British and the Peshwa, Appa Sahib threw off his cloak of friendship, and accepted an embassy and a title from the Peshwa. His troops attacked the British, and were defeated in the action at Sitabuldi, and a second time close to Nagpur city. The remaining portion of Berar and the territories in the Narmada valley were ceded to the British. After the Third Anglo-Maratha War, Nagpur was under a under a subsidiary alliance with the British. Appa Sahib was reinstated to the throne, but shortly afterwards was discovered to be again conspiring, and was deposed and sent to Allahabad in custody. Raghoji II was succeeded by Raghoji III. he ruled Nagpur under a with the British resident Richard Jenkins. Raghoji died on 11 December 1853 without a male heir. Nagpur was annexed by the British under the doctrine of lapse. The former kingdom was administered as Nagpur Province, under a commissioner appointed by then Governor-General of India, James Broun-Ramsay.

- **Thanjavur Maratha kingdom**

The Bhonsoles were also influential in the Carnatic Region. In 1675, the Sultan of Bijapur sent a force commanded by the Maratha general Venkoji a half-brother of the Shivaji, to Capture the city of Thanjavur and Established the Thanjavur Maratha Kingdom. Venkoji defeated Alagiri, and occupied Thanjavur. He did not, however, place his protege on the throne as instructed by the Bijapur Sultan, but seized the kingdom and made himself king. Thus began the rule of the Marathas over Thanjavur. Vyankoji also allied with Chokkanatha of Madurai to repulse an invasion from Mysore.Shivaji Maharaj also invaded Gingee and Thanjavur in 1676–1677 and made his brother Santaji the ruler of all lands to the north of the Coleroon.

FIVE

MARATHA EMPIRE

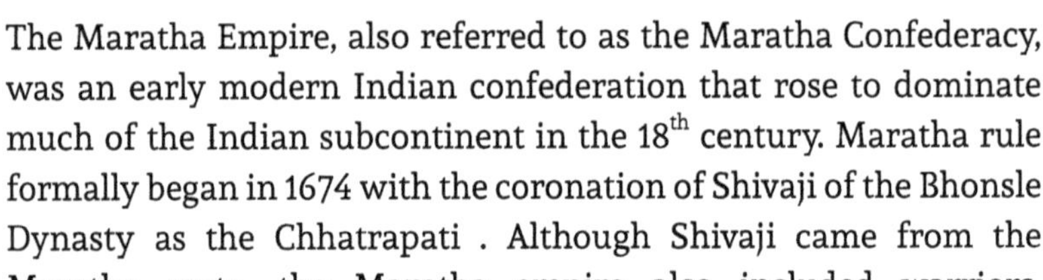

The Maratha Empire, also referred to as the Maratha Confederacy, was an early modern Indian confederation that rose to dominate much of the Indian subcontinent in the 18th century. Maratha rule formally began in 1674 with the coronation of Shivaji of the Bhonsle Dynasty as the Chhatrapati . Although Shivaji came from the Maratha caste, the Maratha empire also included warriors, administrators and other notables from Maratha and several other castes from Maharashtra.

They are largely credited for ending Mughal control over the Indian subcontinent and establishing the Maratha Empire. The religious attitude of Mughal Emperor Aurangzeb estranged non-Muslims, and his inability to finish the resulting Maratha uprising after a 27-year war at a great cost to his men and treasure, eventually ensued Maratha ascendency and control over sizeable portions of former Mughal lands in the north or about 1/3 of the subcontinent by 1757. Maratha rule officially ended in 1818 with the defeat of Peshwa Bajirao II at the hands of the British East India Company in Third Anglo-Maratha War.

The Marathas were a Marathi-speaking warrior group from the western Deccan Plateau. who rose to prominence by establishing Hindavi Swarajya . The Marathas became prominent in the 17th century under the leadership of Shivaji, who revolted against the Adil Shahi dynasty, and the Mughals to carve out a kingdom with

Raigad as his capital.

His father, Shahaji, had earlier conquered Thanjavur which Shivaji's half-brother, Venkoji Rao (alias Ekoji) inherited. This kingdom was known as the Thanjavur Maratha kingdom. Bangalore which was established in 1537 by a vassal of the Vijayanagara Empire, Kempe Gowda I who declared independence, was captured in 1638 by a large Adil Shahi Bijapur army led by Ranadulla Khan who, accompanied by his second in command Shahaji, defeated Kempe Gowda III. As a result, Bangalore was given to Shahaji as a jagir (feudal estate). Known for their mobility, the Marathas were able to consolidate their territory during the Mughal–Maratha Wars and later controlled a large part of the Indian subcontinent.

Upon his release from Mughal captivity, Shahu became the Maratha ruler after a brief struggle with his aunt Tarabai, with the help of Balaji Vishwanath. Pleased by his help, Shahu appointed Balaji and later, his descendants, as the Peshwas or prime ministers of the empire. Balaji and his descendants played a key role in the expansion of Maratha rule. The empire, at its peak in 1758, stretched for a brief time from Tamil Nadu in the south, to Peshawar (modern-day Khyber Pakhtunkhwa, Pakistan) in the north, and Orissa & West Bengal up to the Hooghly River, in the east. However, they lost their occupations beyond Delhi, when the Maratha Army lost the Third Battle of Panipat in 1761. Ten years after Panipat, the young Peshwa Madhav Rao I's Maratha Resurrection reinstated Maratha authority over North India. The Marathas discussed abolishing the Mughal throne and placing Vishwas Rao on it in Delhi.

To effectively manage the large empire, Madhav Rao gave semi-autonomy to the strongest of the knights, creating a confederacy of Maratha states. These leaders became known as the Gaekwads of Baroda, the Holkars of Indore and Malwa, the Scindias of Gwalior and Ujjain, the Bhonsales of Nagpur, the Jadhavs of Vidarbha, the Dabhades of Gujarat, the Puars of Dhar and Dewas. In 1775, the East India Company intervened in a Peshwa family succession struggle in Pune, which led to the First Anglo-Maratha War in which the

Marathas emerged victorious. The Marathas remained the pre-eminent power in India until their defeat in the Second and Third Anglo-Maratha Wars (1805–1818), which resulted in the East India Company seizing control of most of the Indian subcontinent. The Maratha Empire came to an end in 1818, with its last Peshwa being Baji Rao II.

A large portion of the Maratha empire was coastline, which had been secured by the potent Maratha Navy under commanders such as Kanhoji Angre. He successfully kept foreign naval ships at bay, particularly those of the Portuguese and British. Securing the coastal areas and building land-based fortifications were crucial aspects of the Maratha's defensive strategy and regional military history.

The Maratha Empire is also referred to as the Maratha Confederacy. The historian Barbara Ramusack says that the former is a designation preferred by Indian nationalists, while the latter was that used by British historians. She notes, "neither term is fully accurate since one implies a substantial degree of centralisation and the other signifies some surrender of power to a central government and a longstanding core of political administrators".Although at present, the word Maratha refers to a particular caste of warriors and peasants, in the past the word has been used to describe all Marathi people.

- **The Chhatrapati**

The empire had its head in the Chhatrapati as de jure, but the de facto governance was in the hands of the Peshwas after Chhatrapati Shahu I's reign. After the death of Peshwa Madhavrao I, various chiefs played the role of the de facto rulers in their regions.

Shivaji (1630–1680) was a Maratha aristocrat of the Bhosale clan who is the founder of the Maratha empire. Shivaji led a resistance to free the people from the Sultanate of Bijapur in 1645 by winning the fort Torna, followed by many more forts, placing the area under his control and establishing Hindavi Swarajya). He created an independent Maratha kingdom with Raigad as its capital and successfully fought against the Mughals to defend his kingdom. He was crowned as Chhatrapati (sovereign) of the new Maratha kingdom in 1674.

The Maratha dominion under him comprised about 4.1% of the subcontinent, but it was spread over large tracts. At the time of his death, it was reinforced with about 300 forts, and defended by about 40,000 cavalries, and 50,000 soldiers, as well as naval establishments along the west coast. Over time, the kingdom would increase in size and heterogeneity by the time of his grandson's rule, and later under the Peshwas in the early 18th century, it was a full-fledged empire.

- **Sambhaji, eldest son of Shivaji**

Shivaji had two sons: Sambhaji and Rajaram, who had different mothers and were half-brothers. In 1681, Sambhaji succeeded to the crown after his father's death and resumed his expansionist policies. Sambhaji had earlier defeated the Portuguese and Chikka Deva Raya of Mysore. To nullify the alliance between his rebel son, Akbar, and the Marathas, Mughal Emperor Aurangzeb headed south in 1681. With his entire imperial court, administration and an army of about 500,000 troops, he proceeded to expand the Mughal empire, gaining territories such as the sultanates of Bijapur and Golconda. During the eight years that followed, Sambhaji led the Marathas successfully against the Mughals.

In early 1689, Sambhaji called his commanders for a strategic meeting at Sangameshwar to consider an onslaught on the Mughal forces. In a meticulously planned operation, Ganoji and Aurangzeb's commander, Mukarrab Khan, attacked Sangameshwar when Sambhaji was accompanied by just a few men. Sambhaji was ambushed and captured by the Mughal troops on 1 February 1689. He and his advisor, Kavi Kalash, were taken to Bahadurgad by the imperial army, where they were executed by the Mughals on 21 March 1689. Aurangzeb had charged Sambhaji with attacks by

Maratha forces on Burhanpur.

Upon Sambhaji's death, his half-brother Rajaram ascended the throne. The Mughal siege of Raigad continued, and he had to flee to Vishalgad and then to Gingee for safety. From there, the Marathas raided Mughal territory, and many forts were recaptured by Maratha commanders such as Santaji Ghorpade, Dhanaji Jadhav, Parshuram Pant Pratinidhi, Shankaraji Narayan Sacheev and Melgiri Pandit. In 1697, Rajaram offered a truce but this was rejected by Aurangzeb. Rajaram died in 1700 at Sinhagad. His widow, Tarabai, assumed control in the name of her son, Ramaraja (Shivaji II).

After Aurangzeb died in 1707, Shahu, the son of Sambhaji (and grandson of Shivaji), was released by Bahadur Shah I, the new Mughal emperor. However, his mother was kept a hostage of the Mughals to ensure that Shahu adhered to the release conditions. Upon release, Shahu immediately claimed the Maratha throne and challenged his aunt Tarabai and her son. The spluttering Mughal-Maratha war became a three-cornered affair. This resulted in two rival seats of government being set up in 1707 at Satara and Kolhapur by Shahu and Tarabai respectively.

Shahu appointed Balaji Vishwanath as his Peshwa. The Peshwa was instrumental in securing Mughal recognition of Shahu as the rightful heir of Shivaji and the Chhatrapati of the Marathas. Balaji also gained the release of Shahu's mother, Yesubai, from Mughal captivity in 1719.During Shahu's reign, Raghoji Bhosale expanded the empire Eastwards, reaching present-day Bengal. Khanderao Dabhade and later his son, Triambakrao, expanded it Westwards into Gujarat. Peshwa Bajirao and his three chiefs, Pawar (Dhar), Holkar (Indore), and Scindia (Gwalior), expanded it northwards up to Peshawar. He also expanded it up to Kaveri river.

- **Peshwa era**

Shaniwar Wada palace fort in Pune, it was the seat of the Peshwa rulers of the Maratha Empire until 1818.During this era, Peshwas belonging to the Bhat family controlled the Maratha Army and later became de facto rulers of the Maratha Empire till 1772. In due course of time, the Maratha Empire dominated most of the Indian subcontinent.

- **Peshwa Balaji Vishwanath**

Shahu appointed Peshwa Balaji Vishwanath in 1713. From his time, the office of Peshwa became supreme while Shahu became a figurehead. His first major achievement was the conclusion of the Treaty of Lonavala in 1714 with Kanhoji Angre, the most powerful naval chief on the Western Coast. He later accepted Shahu as Chhatrapati. In 1719, Marathas marched to Delhi after defeating Sayyid Hussain Ali, the Mughal governor of Deccan, and deposed the Mughal emperor. The Mughal Emperors became puppets in the hands of their Maratha overlords from this point on.

- **Peshwa Baji Rao I**

After Balaji Vishwanath's death in April 1720, his son, Baji Rao I, was appointed Peshwa by Shahu. Bajirao is credited with expanding the Maratha Empire tenfold from 3% to 30% of the modern Indian landscape during 1720–1740. He fought over 41 battles before his death in April 1740 and is reputed to have never lost any. The Battle of Palkhed was a land battle that took place on 28 February 1728 at the village of Palkhed, near the city of Nashik, Maharashtra, India between Baji Rao I and Qamar-ud-din Khan, Asaf Jah I of Hyderabad. The Marathas defeated the Nizam. The battle is considered an example of the brilliant execution of military strategy.

In 1737, Marathas under Bajirao I raided the suburbs of Delhi in a blitzkrieg in the Battle of Delhi (1737). The Nizam set out from the Deccan to rescue the Mughals from the invasion of the Marathas, but was defeated decisively in the Battle of Bhopal. The Marathas extracted a large tribute from the Mughals and signed a treaty which ceded Malwa to the Marathas. The Battle of Vasai was fought between the Marathas and the Portuguese rulers of Vasai, a village lying on the northern shore of Vasai creek, 50 km north of Mumbai. The Marathas were led by Chimaji Appa, brother of Baji Rao. The Maratha victory in this war was a major achievement of Baji Rao's time in office.

- **Peshwa Balaji Bajirao**

Baji Rao's son, Balaji Bajirao (Nanasaheb), was appointed as the next Peshwa by Shahu despite the opposition of other chiefs. In 1740, the Maratha forces, under Raghoji Bhosale, came down upon Arcot and defeated the Nawab of Arcot, Dost Ali, in the pass at Damalcherry. In the war that followed, Dost Ali, one of his sons Hasan Ali, and a number of other prominent persons lost their lives. This initial success at once enhanced Maratha prestige in the south. From Damalcherry, the Marathas proceeded to Arcot, which surrendered to them without much resistance. Then, Raghuji invaded Trichinopoly in December 1740. Unable to resist, Chanda Sahib surrendered the fort to Raghuji on 14 March 1741. Chanda Saheb and his son were arrested and sent to Nagpur. Rajputana also came under Maratha domination during this time. In June 1756 Luís Mascarenhas, Count of Alva (Conde de Alva), the Portuguese Viceroy was killed in action by the Maratha Army in Goa.

After the successful campaign of Karnataka and the Trichinopolly, Raghuji returned from Karnataka. He undertook six expeditions into Bengal from 1741 to 1748.The resurgent Maratha Empire launched brutal raids against the prosperous Bengali state in the 18th century, which further added to the decline of the Nawabs of Bengal. During their invasions and occupation of Bihar and western Bengal up to the Hooghly River, During their occupation of western Bengal, the Marathas perpetrated atrocities against the local population. The Maratha atrocities were recorded by both Bengali and European sources, which reported that the Marathas demanded payments, and tortured or killed anyone who couldn't pay.

Raghuji was able to annex Odisha to his kingdom permanently as he successfully exploited the chaotic conditions prevailing in Bengal after the death of its governor Murshid Quli Khan in 1727. Constantly harassed by the Bhonsles, Odisha, Bengal and parts of Bihar were economically ruined. Alivardi Khan, the Nawab of Bengal made peace with Raghuji in 1751 ceding Cuttack (Odisha) up to the river Subarnarekha, and agreeing to pay Rs. 1.2 million annually as the Chauth for Bengal and Bihar.

Balaji Bajirao encouraged agriculture, protected the villagers and brought about a marked improvement in the state of the territory. Raghunath Rao, brother of Nanasaheb, pushed into the wake of the Afghan withdrawal after Ahmed Shah Abdali's plunder of Delhi in 1756. Delhi was captured by the Maratha army under Raghunath Rao in August 1757, defeating the Afghan garrison in the Battle of Delhi. This laid the foundation for the Maratha conquest of North-west India. In Lahore, as in Delhi, the Marathas were now major players. After the 1758 Battle of Attock, the Marathas captured Peshawar defeating the Afghan troops in the Battle of Peshawar on 8 May 1758.

Just prior to the battle of Panipat in 1761, the Marathas looted "Diwan-i-Khas" or Hall of Private Audiences in the Red Fort of Delhi, which was the place where the Mughal emperors used to receive courtiers and state guests, in one of their expeditions to Delhi.The Marathas who were hard pressed for money stripped the ceiling of Diwan-i-Khas of its silver and looted the shrines dedicated to Muslim maulanas.

- **During the Maratha invasion of Rohilkhand in the 1750s**

The Marathas defeated the Rohillas, forced them to seek shelter in hills and ransacked their country in such a manner that the Rohillas dreaded the Marathas and hated them ever afterwards.

In 1760, the Marathas under Sadashivrao Bhau responded to the news of the Afghans' return to North India by sending a large army north. Bhau's force was bolstered by some Maratha forces under Holkar, Scindia, Gaikwad and Govind Pant Bundele with Suraj Mal. The combined army of over 50,000 regular troops re-captured the former Mughal capital, Delhi, from an Afghan garrison in August 1760.Delhi had been reduced to ashes many times due to previous invasions, and there was an acute shortage of supplies in the Maratha camp. Bhau ordered the sacking of the already depopulated city. He is said to have planned to place his nephew and the Peshwa's son, Vishwasrao, on the Mughal throne. By 1760, with defeat of the Nizam in the Deccan, Maratha power had reached its zenith with a territory of over 2,500,000 square kilometres (970,000 sq mi).

Ahmad Shah Durrani called on the Rohillas and the Nawab of Oudh to assist him in driving out the Marathas from Delhi. Huge armies of Muslim forces and Marathas collided with each other on 14 January 1761 in the Third Battle of Panipat. The Maratha Army lost the battle, which halted their imperial expansion. The Jats and Rajputs did not support the Marathas. Historians have criticised the Maratha treatment of fellow Hindu groups. Kaushik Roy says "The treatment of Marathas with their co-religionist fellows – Jats and Rajputs was definitely unfair After the battle, Malhar Rao Holkar attacked the Rajputs and defeated them at the battle of Mangrol. This largely restored Maratha power in Rajasthan.

The Marathas had antagonised the Jats and Rajputs by taxing them heavily, punishing them after defeating the Mughals and interfering in their internal affairs. The Marathas were abandoned by Raja Suraj Mal of Bharatpur, who quit the Maratha alliance at Agra before the start of the great battle and withdrew their troops as Maratha general Sadashivrao Bhau did not heed the advice to leave soldier's families (women and children) and pilgrims at Agra and not take them to the battle field with the soldiers, rejected their co-operation. Their supply chains (earlier assured by Raja Suraj Mal) did not exist.

- **Peshwa Madhavrao I**

Peshwa Madhavrao I was the fourth Peshwa of the Maratha Empire. It was during his tenure that the Maratha Resurrection took place. He worked as a unifying force in the Maratha Empire and moved to the south to subdue Mysore and the Nizam of Hyderabad to assert Maratha power. He sent generals such as Bhonsle, Scindia and Holkar to the north, where they re-established Maratha authority by the early 1770s. Madhav Rao I crossed the Krishna River in 1767 and defeated Hyder Ali in the battles of Sira and Madgiri. He also rescued the last queen of the Keladi Nayaka Kingdom, who had been kept in confinement by Hyder Ali in the fort of Madgiri.

- **Maratha king of Gwalior at his palace**

In early 1771, ten years after the collapse of Maratha authority over North India following the Third Battle of Panipat, Mahadji recaptured Delhi and installed Shah Alam II as a puppet ruler on the Mughal throne receiving in return the title of deputy Vakil-ul-Mutlak or vice-regent of the Empire and that of Vakil-ul-Mutlak being at his request conferred on the Peshwa. The Mughals also gave him the title of Amir-ul-Amara (head of the amirs). After taking control of Delhi, the Marathas sent a large army in 1772 to punish Afghan Rohillas for their involvement in Panipat. Their army devastated Rohilkhand by looting and plundering as well as taking members of the royal family as captives.Madhav Rao died in 1772, at the age of 27. His death is considered to be a fatal blow to the Maratha Empire and from that time Maratha power started to move on a downward trajectory, less an empire than a confederacy.

In a bid to effectively manage the large empire, Madhavrao Peshwa gave semi-autonomy to the strongest of the aristocracy. After the death of Peshwa Madhavrao I, various chiefs and jagirdars became de facto rulers and regents for the infant Peshwa Madhavrao II. Under the leadership of Mahadji Shinde, the ruler of the state of Gwalior in central India, the Marathas defeated the Jats, the Rohilla Afghans and took Delhi which remained under Maratha control for the next three decades. His forces conquered modern day Haryana. Shinde was instrumental in resurrecting Maratha power after the débâcle of the Third Battle of Panipat, and in this he was assisted by Benoît de Boigne.

After the growth in power of feudal lords like Malwa sardars, landlords of Bundelkhand and Rajput kingdoms of Rajasthan, they refused to pay tribute to Mahadji, so he sent his army to conquer the states such as Bhopal, Datiya, Chanderi, Narwar, Salbai and Gohad. However, he launched an unsuccessful expedition against the Raja of Jaipur, but withdrew after the inconclusive Battle of Lalsot in 1787. The Battle of Gajendragad was fought between the Marathas under the command of Tukojirao Holkar (the adopted son of Malharrao Holkar) and Tipu Sultan from March 1786 to March 1787 in which Tipu Sultan was defeated by the Marathas. By the victory in this battle, the border of the Maratha territory extended till Tungabhadra river. The strong fort of Gwalior was then in the hands of Chhatar Singh, the Jat ruler of Gohad. In 1783, Mahadji besieged the fort of Gwalior and conquered it. He delegated the administration of Gwalior to Khanderao Hari Bhalerao. After celebrating the conquest of Gwalior, Mahadji Shinde turned his attention to Delhi again.

In 1788, Mahadji's armies defeated Ismail Beg, a Mughal noble who resisted the Marathas. The Rohilla chief Ghulam Kadir, Ismail Beg's ally, took over Delhi, capital of the Mughal dynasty and deposed and blinded the king Shah Alam II, placing a puppet on the Delhi throne. Mahadji intervened and killed him, taking possession of Delhi on 2 October restoring Shah Alam II to the throne and acting as his protector. Jaipur and Jodhpur, the two most powerful Rajput states, were still out of direct Maratha domination. So, Mahadji sent his general Benoît de Boigne to crush the forces of Jaipur and Jodhpur at the Battle of Patan. Marwar was also captured on 10 September 1790. Another achievement of the Marathas was their victories over the Nizam of Hyderabad's armies including in the Battle of Kharda.

- **Maratha–Mysore Wars**

The Marathas came into conflict with Tipu Sultan and his Kingdom of Mysore, leading to the Maratha–Mysore War in 1785. The war ended in 1787 with the Tipu Sultan being defeated by Marathas. The Maratha-Mysore war ended in April 1787, following the finalizing of the treaty of Gajendragad, as per which, Tipu Sultan of Mysore was obligated to pay 4.8 million rupees as a war cost to the Marathas, and an annual tribute of 1.2 million rupees, in addition to returning all the territory captured by Hyder Ali, In 1791–92, large areas of the Maratha Confederacy suffered massive population loss due to the Doji bara famine.

In 1791, irregulars like lamaans and pindaris of the Maratha army raided and looted the temple of Sringeri Shankaracharya, killing and wounding many people including Brahmins, plundering the monastery of all its valuable possessions, and desecrating the temple by displacing the image of goddess Sāradā. The incumbent Shankaracharya petitioned Tipu Sultan for help. A bunch of about 30 letters written in Kannada, which were exchanged between Tipu Sultan's court and the Sringeri Shankaracharya were discovered in 1916 by the Director of Archaeology in Mysore.

Tipu Sultan immediately ordered the Asaf of Bednur to supply the Swami with 200 rahatis (fanams) in cash and other gifts and articles. Tipu Sultan's interest in the Sringeri temple continued for many years, and he was still writing to the Swami in the 1790s.

The Maratha Empire soon allied with the British East India Company (based in the Bengal Presidency) against Mysore in the Anglo-Mysore Wars. After the British had suffered defeat against Mysore in the first two Anglo-Mysore Wars, the Maratha cavalry assisted the British in the last two Anglo-Mysore Wars from 1790 onwards, eventually helping the British conquer Mysore in the Fourth Anglo-Mysore War in 1799. After the British conquest, however, the Marathas launched frequent raids in Mysore to plunder the region, which they justified as compensation for past losses to Tipu Sultan.

In 1775, the British East India Company, from its base in Bombay, intervened in a succession struggle in Pune, on behalf of Raghunathrao (also called Raghobadada), who wanted to become Peshwa of the empire. Marathas forces under Tukojirao Holkar and Mahadaji Shinde defeated a British expeditionary force at the Battle of Wadgaon, but the heavy surrender terms, which included the return of annexed territory and a share of revenues, were disavowed by the British authorities at Bengal and fighting continued. What became known as the First Anglo-Maratha War ended in 1782 with a restoration of the pre-war status quo and the East India Company's abandonment of Raghunathrao's cause.

- **Peshwa Madhavrao II in his court in 1790, concluding a treaty with the British**

In 1799, Yashwantrao Holkar was crowned King of the Holkars and he captured Ujjain. He started campaigning towards the north to expand his empire in that region. Yashwant Rao rebelled against the policies of Peshwa Baji Rao II. In May 1802, he marched towards Pune the seat of the Peshwa. This gave rise to the Battle of Poona in which the Peshwa was defeated.

After the Battle of Poona, the flight of the Peshwa left the government of the Maratha state in the hands of Yashwantrao Holkar.(Kincaid & Pārasanīsa 1925, p. 194) He appointed Amrutrao as the Peshwa and went to Indore on 13 March 1803. All except Gaikwad, chief of Baroda, who had already accepted British protection by a separate treaty on 26 July 1802, supported the new regime. He made a treaty with the British. Also, Yashwant Rao successfully resolved the disputes with Scindia and the Peshwa. He tried to unite the Maratha Confederacy but to no avail.

In 1802, the British intervened in Baroda to support the heir to the throne against rival claimants and they signed a treaty with the new Maharaja recognising his independence from the Maratha Empire in return for his acknowledgment of British paramountcy. Before the Second Anglo-Maratha War (1803–1805), the Peshwa Baji

Rao II signed a similar treaty. The defeat in Battle of Delhi, 1803 during the Second Anglo-Maratha War resulted in the loss of the city of Delhi for the Marathas.

The Second Anglo-Maratha War represents the military high-water mark of the Marathas who posed the last serious opposition to the formation of the British Raj. The real contest for India was never a single decisive battle for the subcontinent. Rather, it turned on a complex social and political struggle for the control of the South Asian military economy. The victory in 1803 hinged as much on finance, diplomacy, politics and intelligence as it did on battlefield maneuver and war itself.

- **Battle of Assaye during the Second Anglo-Maratha War**

Ultimately, the Third Anglo-Maratha War (1817–1818) resulted in the loss of Maratha independence. It left the British in control of most of the Indian subcontinent. The Peshwa was exiled to Bithoor (Marat, near Kanpur, Uttar Pradesh) as a pensioner of the British. The Maratha heartland of Desh, including Pune, came under direct British rule, with the exception of the states of Kolhapur and Satara, which retained local Maratha rulers (descendants of Shivaji and Sambhaji II ruled over Kolhapur). The Maratha-ruled states of Gwalior, Indore, and Nagpur all lost territory and came under subordinate alliances with the British Raj as princely states that retained internal sovereignty under British paramountcy. Other small princely states of Maratha knights were retained under the British Raj as well.

- **Peshwa Baji Rao II signing of the Treaty of Bassein with the British**

The Third Anglo-Maratha War was fought by Maratha warlords separately instead of forming a common front and they surrendered one by one. Shinde and the Pashtun Amir Khan were subdued by the use of diplomacy and pressure, which resulted in the Treaty of Gwalior on 5 November 1817. All other Maratha chiefs like Holkars, Bhonsles and the Peshwa gave up arms by 1818. British historian Percival Spear describes 1818 as a watershed year in the history of India, saying that by that year "the British dominion in India became the British dominion of India".

The war left the British, under the auspices of the British East India Company, in control of virtually all of present-day India south of the Sutlej River. The famed Nassak Diamond was looted by the company as part of the spoils of the war. The British acquired large chunks of territory from the Maratha Empire and in effect put an end to their most dynamic opposition. The terms of surrender Major-general John Malcolm offered to the Peshwa were controversial amongst the British for being too liberal: The Peshwa was offered a luxurious life near Kanpur and given a pension of about 80,000 pounds.In 1760, the peace of Peshwa government was broken by a rising of Kolis under their Naik Javji Bamble. Javji with drew to the hills and organised a series of gang robberies, causing widespread terror and misery throughout the country. For twenty years he held out bravely, defeating and killing the generals of the Peshwa's Government sent against him.

At last he was so hotly pursued that, on the advice of Dhondo Gopal, the Peshwa's governor at Nasik, he surrendered all his forts to Tukoji Holkar and, through Holkar's influence, was pardoned and placed in military and police charge of a district of sixty villages with powers of life and death outlaws. In 1798, a fresh disturbance took place among the Kolis. The leader of this outbreak was Ramji Naik Bhangria, who was an abler and more daring man than his prede cessors, and succeeded in baffling all the efforts of the Government officers to seize him. As force seemed hopeless, the Government offered Ramji a pardon and gave him an important police post.

In 1763, the Peshwa Raghunathrao had appointed Abha Purandare who was an anti koli as Sarnaik, due to which the Chivhe Kolis revolted against the Peshwa and captured Purandar and Sinhagad forts because the Kolis did not like Abha Purandare, so

Abha removed the Kolis from the fortification and posted new Kiledars, due to which the Kolis attacked and captured the forts on 7 May 1764. Five days later, Rudramal fort was also captured and presented a challenge to the Prime Minister of the Maratha Empire, Peshwa Raghunathrao.

A few days later the Peshwa came to the fort to worship the deity inside the Purandar fort but the Peshwa got caught up by the Kolis. The Kolis looted all the belongings and weapons of the Peshwa and took him prisoner but released after some time. After this the Kolis started collecting revenue from the surrounding area. After this, the chief of the Kolis, Kondaji Chivhe, sent a letter to the Peshwa, in which it was written 'What now sir, what is the condition, how is the government doing, be in fun'. After reading this letter, the Peshwa felt a bit humiliated and in a fit of rage ordered the Maratha army to attack but the army could not do anything because the Kolis himselves were Subedar and had fortified the forts well and the Peshwa faced failure. the humiliated Peshwa started taking the Kolis of Chivhe clan as captive. All those Chivhe kolis who were living in the territory of Peshwa were declared as rebels and started making captives. After this the Chivhe Kolis sent a letter to Madhavrao and explained whole matter, after this the Kolis handed over the forts to Madhavrao and the Chivahe Kolis were again handed over the fortifications.

In the year 1776, a large number of the Shelkande Kolis of Otur village, raised against Peshwa because of their hereditary land rights and as the Peshwa refused to do them. Kolis assembled a revolutionary army of Shelkande and Kokate Kolis and commenced plundering the surrounding villages and doing other violent activities in the hope of obtaining redress.

In response, The Peshwa sent Maratha troops from Pune against rebel kolis and surprised them, killed and wounded many of them. The Koli leaders were consequently forced to disperse the rebels. The government officers learned that Sattu Shelkande, chief of the insurgents, was hiding in the neighboring jungle. The better to ensure this, they obliged him to enter into the Sunkli zamin or chain security. Hearing of the measures the government officers were adopting, moved off to another place; this was partly for their own safety, and partly to save their friends from being harassed and punished for not fulfilling their promise of apprehending them. After the troops retired from the jungles, the Kolis recommenced their operations. Several seasons were passed in this way; however when Javji Bamble was appointed as Mansabdar of Rajur he was ordered by Peshwa to prevent the rebellious activities by rebels. Kolis did not wish to fight with Bumble because he was also a Koli by caste.

Kolis remained quiet for four years but Kolis went again to the jungles because his hereditary rights have not been fulfilled. The troops employed against the Shelkande Kolis and again forced them to disperse and the chiefs went to Aurangabad. Kolis had taken an oath that they would cut off the head of Patil of Otur, unless Peshwa afforded them redress.

Nana Phadnavis who was minister in Maratha Empire declared that he would not pardon the Kolis again, as they were such a turbulent race and as no faith could be reposed in them. Nana Fadnavis detached few Brahmins disguised as Gusai, who gained information of the hiding place of Kolis and a detachment that marched to apprehend them was so fortunate as to bring them all prisoners to Junnar, where the five Kolis were executed. Balwantrao, brother-in-law to Nana Fadnavis, was subedar of the district at the time, and it is asserted Balwantrao became very unhappy after the execution of these kolis. Therefore, in the hope of reestablishing the happiness that he had enjoyed, he erected a temple near river in Junnar, in which was placed as the object of worship a Punah Lingh, or five stones representing the five Kolis who were executed.

The Maratha Empire, at its peak, encompassed a large area of the Indian sub-continent. The Maratha Empire at its zenith, expanded from Afghanistan in the north to Thanjavur in the south, Sindh in the west to Bengal in the east. It bordered Nepal and Afghanistan in the north. Apart from capturing various regions, the Marathas maintained a large number of tributaries who were bounded by agreements to pay a certain amount of regular tax, known as Chauth. The empire defeated the Sultanate of Mysore under Hyder Ali and Tipu Sultan, the Nawab of Oudh, the Nizam of Hyderabad, the Nawab of Bengal, Nawab of Sindh and the Nawab of Arcot as well as the Polygar kingdoms of South India. They extracted chauth from the rulers in Delhi, Oudh, Bengal, Bihar, Odisha, Punjab, Kumaon, Garhwal, Hyderabad, Mysore, Uttar Pradesh, Sindh and Rajputana. They built up the largest Hindu empire in India after the fall of the Gupta Empire on the 6th century.

The Mahratta Country, consists of two grand parts, the Poonah or Western division, and the Berar or Eastern division, it extends from Delhi in the north, to the Krishna River in the south, and from the Gulf of Bengal in the east, to the Gulf of Arabia in the west, embracing a territory One Thousand miles from east to west, and Nine hundred miles from north to south, taken in the longest parts; Poonah is the capital of the Western division, and Nagpour of the Eastern: It is governed by many princes, under a Chief called the Peishwah, whose authority is similar to that of the German Emperor: These states are not only the most powerful, but the most warlike of all nations of India.

The Marathas were requested by Safdarjung, the Nawab of Oudh, in 1752 to help him defeat the Afghani Rohillas. The Maratha force set out from Pune and defeated the Afghan Rohillas in 1752, capturing the whole of Rohilkhand (present-day northwestern Uttar Pradesh).In 1752, the Marathas entered into an agreement with the Mughal emperor, through his wazir, Safdarjung, and the Mughals gave the Marathas the chauth of Punjab, Sindh and Doab in addition to the Subahdari of Ajmer and Agra. In 1758, Marathas started their north-west conquest and expanded their boundary till Afghanistan. They defeated Afghan forces of Ahmed Shah Abdali, in what is now Pakistan, including Pakistani Punjab Province and Khyber Pakhtunkhwa. The Afghans were numbered around 25,000–30,000 and were led by Timur Shah, the son of Ahmad Shah Durrani. The Marathas massacred and looted thousands of Afghan soldiers and captured Lahore, Multan, Dera Ghazi Khan, Attock,

Peshawar in the Punjab region and Kashmir. They also made sporadic raids in Afghanistan.

During the confederacy era, Mahadji Shinde resurrected the Maratha domination on much of North India, which was lost after the Third battle of Panipat including the cis-Sutlej states (south of Sutlej) like Kaithal, Patiala, Jind, Thanesar, Maler Kotla and Faridkot. Delhi and much of Uttar Pradesh were under the suzerainty of the Scindhias of the Maratha Empire, but following the Second Anglo-Maratha War of 1803–1805, the Marathas lost these territories to the British East India Company. The empire even after the defeat at Panipat expanded from Punjab in the north to Karnataka in the south.

The Peshwa was the titular equivalent of a modern Prime Minister. Shivaji created the Peshwa designation in order to more effectively delegate administrative duties during the growth of the Maratha Empire. Prior to 1749, Peshwas held office for 8–9 years and controlled the Maratha Army. They later became the de facto hereditary administrators of the Maratha Empire from 1749 till its end in 1818.

Under the administration of the Peshwas and with the support of several key generals and diplomats (listed below), the Maratha Empire reached its zenith, ruling most of the Indian subcontinent. It was also under the Peshwas that the Maratha Empire came to its end through its formal annexation into the British Empire by the British East India Company in 1818.The Marathas used a secular policy of administration and allowed complete freedom of religion.

Shivaji was an able administrator who established a government that included modern concepts such as cabinet, foreign policy and internal intelligence. He established an effective civil and military administration. He believed that there was a close bond between the state and the citizens. He is remembered as a just and welfare-minded king. Cosme da Guarda says of him that Such was the good treatment Shivaji accorded to people and such was the honesty with which he observed the capitulations that none looked upon him without a feeling of love and confidence.

By his people he was exceedingly loved. Both in matters of reward and punishment he was so impartial that while he lived he made no exception for any person; no merit was left unrewarded, no offence went unpunished; and this he did with so much care and attention that he specially charged his governors to inform him in writing of the conduct of his soldiers, mentioning in particular those who had distinguished themselves, and he would at once order their promotion, either in rank or in pay, according to their merit. He was naturally loved by all men of valor and good conduct.

The Marathas carried out a number of sea raids, such as plundering Mughal Naval ships and European trading vessels. European traders described these attacks as piracy, but the Marathas viewed them as legitimate targets because they were trading with, and thus financially supporting, their Mughal and Bijapur enemies. After the representatives of various European powers signed agreements with Shivaji or his successors, the threat of plundering or raids against Europeans began to reduce.

- **Maratha Gurabs ships attacking a British East India Company ship**

The Maratha army, especially its infantry, was praised by almost all the enemies of the Maratha Empire, ranging from the Duke of Wellington to Ahmad Shah Abdali. After the Third Battle of Panipat, Abdali was relieved as the Maratha army in the initial stages were almost in the position of destroying the Afghan armies and their Indian Allies, the Nawab of Oudh and Rohillas. The grand wazir of the Durrani Empire, Sardar Shah Wali Khan was shocked when Maratha commander-in-chief Sadashivrao Bhau launched a fierce assault on the centre of Afghan Army, over 10,000 Durrani soldiers were killed alongside Haji Atai Khan, one of the chief commander of Afghan army and nephew of wazir Shah Wali Khan. Such was the fierce assault of the Maratha infantry in hand-to-hand combat that Afghan armies started to flee and the wazir in desperation and rage shouted, "Comrades Whither do you fly, our country is far off".

Post battle, Ahmad Shah Abdali in a letter to one Indian ruler claimed that Afghans were able to defeat the Marathas only because of the blessings of almighty and any other army would have been destroyed by the Maratha army on that particular day even though the Maratha army was numerically inferior to the Afghan army and its Indian allies. Though Abdali won the battle, he also had heavy casualties on his side. So, he sought immediate peace with the Marathas. Abdali wrote in his letter to Peshwa on 10 February 1761:

There is no reason to have animosity amongst us. Your son Vishwasrao and your brother Sadashivrao died in battle – it was unfortunate. Bhau started the battle, so I had to fight back unwillingly. Yet I feel sorry for his death. Please continue your guardianship of Delhi as before, to that I have no opposition. Only let Punjab until Sutlaj remain with us. Reinstate Shah Alam on Delhi's throne as you did before and let there be peace and friendship between us, this is my ardent desire. Please grant me that desire.

- **Arms of Maratha**

Similarly, the Duke of Wellington, after defeating the Marathas, noted that the Marathas, though poorly led by their Generals, had regular infantry and artillery that matched the level of that of the Europeans and warned other British officers from underestimating the Marathas on the battlefield. He cautioned one British general: "You must never allow Maratha infantry to attack head on or in close hand-to-hand combat as in that your army will cover itself with utter disgrace". Even when Arthur Wellesley, 1st Duke of Wellington, became the Prime Minister of Britain, he held the Maratha infantry in utmost respect, claiming it to be one of the best in the world. However, at the same time, he noted the poor leadership of Maratha Generals, who were often responsible for their defeats. Charles Metcalfe, one of the ablest of the British Officials in India and later acting Governor-General, wrote in 1806.

India contains no more than two great powers, British and Mahratta, and every other state acknowledges the influence of one or the other. Every inch that we recede will be occupied by them.Norman Gash says that the Maratha infantry was equal to that of British infantry. After the Third Anglo-Maratha war in 1818, Britain listed the Marathas as one of the Martial Races to serve in the British Indian Army. The 19th-century diplomat Sir Justin Sheil commented about the British East India Company copying the French Indian army in raising an army of Indians:

It is to the military genius of the French that we are indebted for the formation of the Indian army. Our warlike neighbours were the first to introduce into India the system of drilling native troops and converting them into a regularly disciplined force. Their example was copied by us, and the result is what we now behold. The French carried to Persia the same military and administrative faculties, and established the origin of the present Persian regular army, as it is styled. When Napoleon the Great resolved to take Iran under his auspices, he dispatched several officers of superior intelligence to that country with the mission of General Gardanne in 1808. Those gentlemen commenced their operations in the provinces of Azerbaijan and Kermanshah, and it is said with considerable success.

SIX

The Credit Of Mughal Empire

The Mughal Empire was an early-modern empire that controlled much of South Asia between the 16th and 19th centuries. For some two hundred years, the empire stretched from the outer fringes of the Indus river basin in the west, northern Afghanistan in the northwest, and Kashmir in the north, to the highlands of present-day Assam and Bangladesh in the east, and the uplands of the Deccan Plateau in South India.

The Mughal empire is conventionally said to have been founded in 1526 by Babur, a warrior chieftain from what is today Uzbekistan, who employed aid from the neighboring Safavid and Ottoman empires, to defeat the Sultan of Delhi, Ibrahim Lodi, in the First Battle of Panipat, and to sweep down the plains of North India. The Mughal imperial structure, however, is sometimes dated to 1600, to the rule of Babur's grandson, Akbar. This imperial structure lasted until 1720, until shortly after the death of the last major emperor, Aurangzeb, during whose reign the empire also achieved its maximum geographical extent. Reduced subsequently to the region in and around Old Delhi by 1760, the empire was formally dissolved by the British Raj after the Indian Rebellion of 1857.

Although the Mughal empire was created and sustained by military warfare, it did not vigorously suppress the cultures and peoples it came to rule; rather it equalized and placated them through new administrative practices, and diverse ruling elites, leading to more efficient, centralised, and standardized rule. The base of the empire's collective wealth was agricultural taxes, instituted by the third Mughal emperor, Akbar. These taxes, which amounted to well over half the output of a peasant cultivator, were paid in the well-regulated silver currency, and caused peasants and artisans to enter larger markets.

The relative peace maintained by the empire during much of the 17th century was a factor in India's economic expansion. Burgeoning European presence in the Indian Ocean, and its increasing demand for Indian raw and finished products, created still greater wealth in the Mughal courts.There was more conspicuous consumption among the Mughal elite, resulting in greater patronage of painting, literary forms, textiles, and architecture, especially during the reign of Shah Jahan. Among the Mughal UNESCO World Heritage Sites in South Asia are: Agra Fort, Fatehpur Sikri, Red Fort, Humayun's Tomb, Lahore Fort, Shalamar Gardens and the Taj Mahal, which is described as "the jewel of Muslim art in India, and one of the universally admired masterpieces of the world's heritage."

Contemporaries referred to the empire founded by Babur as the Timurid Empire, which reflected the heritage of his dynasty, and this was the term preferred by the Mughals themselves.The Mughal designation for their own dynasty was Gurkani (romanized: Gūrkāniyān, lit. 'sons-in-law'). The use of "Mughal" and "Moghul" derived from the Arabic and Persian corruption of "Mongol", and it emphasised the Mongol origins of the Timurid dynasty. The term gained currency during the 19th century, but remains disputed by Indologists. Similar transliterations had been used to refer to the empire, including "Mogul" and "Moghul". Nevertheless, Babur's ancestors were sharply distinguished from the classical Mongols insofar as they were oriented towards Persian rather than Turco-Mongol culture. The Mughals themselves claimed ultimate descent from Mongol Empire founder Genghis Khan.

Another name for the empire was Hindustan, which was documented in the Ain-i-Akbari, and which has been described as the closest to an official name for the empire. In the west, the term "Mughal" was used for the emperor, and by extension, the empire as a whole.

The Mughal Empire was founded by Babur (reigned 1526–1530), a Central Asian ruler who was descended from the Turco-Mongol conqueror Timur (the founder of the Timurid Empire) on his father's side, and from Genghis Khan on his mother's side. Ousted from his ancestral domains in Central Asia, Babur turned to India to satisfy his ambitions. He established himself in Kabul and then pushed steadily southward into India from Afghanistan through the Khyber Pass.

Babur's forces defeated Ibrahim Lodi in the First Battle of Panipat. Before the battle, Babur sought divine favour by abjuring liquor, breaking the wine vessels and pouring the wine down a well. However, by this time Lodi's empire was already crumbling, and it was actually the Rajput Confederacy which was the strongest power of Northern India under the capable rule of Rana Sanga of Mewar. He defeated Babar in the Battle of Bayana. However, in the decisive Battle of Khanwa which was fought near Agra, the Timurid forces of Babur defeated the Rajput army of Sanga. This battle was one of the most decisive and historic battles in Indian history, as it sealed the fate of Northern India for the next two centuries.

After the battle, the centre of Mughal power became Agra instead of Kabul. The preoccupation with wars and military campaigns, however, did not allow the new emperor to consolidate the gains he had made in India. The instability of the empire became evident under his son, Humayun (reigned 1530–1556), who was forced into exile in Persia by rebels. The Sur Empire (1540–1555), founded by Sher Shah Suri (reigned 1540–1545), briefly interrupted Mughal rule. Humayun's exile in Persia established diplomatic ties between the Safavid and Mughal Courts, and led to increasing Persian cultural influence in the later restored Mughal Empire.Humayun's triumphant return from Persia in 1555 restored Mughal rule in some parts of India, but he died in an accident the next year.

- **Akbar, Jahangir, Shah Jahan, and Aurangzeb**

Akbar (reigned 1556–1605) was born Jalal-ud-din Muhammad in the Rajput Umarkot Fort, to Humayun and his wife Hamida Banu Begum, a Persian princess. Akbar succeeded to the throne under a regent, Bairam Khan, who helped consolidate the Mughal Empire in India. Through warfare and diplomacy, Akbar was able to extend the empire in all directions and controlled almost the entire Indian subcontinent north of the Godavari River. He created a new ruling elite loyal to him, implemented a modern administration, and encouraged cultural developments. He increased trade with European trading companies. India developed a strong and stable economy, leading to commercial expansion and economic development. Akbar allowed freedom of religion at his court, and attempted to resolve socio-political and cultural differences in his empire by establishing a new religion, Din-i-Ilahi, with strong characteristics of a ruler cult. He left his son an internally stable state, which was in the midst of its golden age, but before long signs of political weakness would emerge.

Jahangir (born Salim, reigned 1605–1627) was born to Akbar and his wife Mariam-uz-Zamani, an Indian Rajput princess. Salim was named after the Indian Sufi saint, Salim Chishti and was raised by the daughter of Chishti. He "was addicted to opium, neglected the affairs of the state, and came under the influence of rival court cliques". Jahangir distinguished himself from Akbar by making substantial efforts to gain the support of the Islamic religious establishment. One way he did this was by bestowing many more madad-i-ma'ash than Akbar had. In contrast to Akbar, Jahangir came into conflict with non-Muslim religious leaders, notably the Sikh guru Arjan, whose execution was the first of many conflicts between the Mughal empire and the Sikh community.

Group portrait of Mughal rulers, from Babur to Aurangzeb, with the Mughal ancestor Timur seated in the middle. On the left: Shah

Jahan, Akbar and Babur, with Abu Sa'id of Samarkand and Timur's son, Miran Shah. On the right: Aurangzeb, Jahangir and Humayun, and two of Timur's other offspring Umar Shaykh and Muhammad Sultan. Created c. 1707–12

Shah Jahan (reigned 1628–1658) was born to Jahangir and his wife Jagat Gosain, a Rajput princess. His reign ushered in the golden age of Mughal architecture. During the reign of Shah Jahan, the splendour of the Mughal court reached its peak, as exemplified by the Taj Mahal.The cost of maintaining the court, however, began to exceed the revenue coming in. His reign was called as "The Golden Age of Mughal Architecture". Shah Jahan extended the Mughal empire to the Deccan by ending the Nizam Shahi dynasty, and forced the Adil Shahis and Qutb Shahis to pay tribute.

Shah Jahan's eldest son, the liberal Dara Shikoh, became regent in 1658, as a result of his father's illness. Dara championed a syncretistic Hindu-Muslim culture, emulating his great-grandfather Akbar. With the support of the Islamic orthodoxy, however, a younger son of Shah Jahan, Aurangzeb (r. 1658–1707), seized the throne. Aurangzeb defeated Dara in 1659 and had him executed. Although Shah Jahan fully recovered from his illness, Aurangzeb kept Shah Jahan imprisoned until his death in 1666.Aurangzeb oversaw an increase in the Islamicization of the Mughal state. He encouraged conversion to Islam, reinstated the jizya on non-Muslims, and compiled the Fatawa 'Alamgiri, a collection of Islamic law.

Aurangzeb also ordered the execution of the Sikh guru Tegh Bahadur, leading to the militarization of the Sikh community.From the imperial perspective, conversion to Islam integrated local elites into the king's vision of network of shared identity that would join disparate groups throughout the empire in obedience to the Mughal emperor. He expanded the empire to include almost the whole of South Asia but at his death in 1707, "many parts of the empire were in open revolt". Aurangzeb is considered India's most controversial king, with some historians arguing his religious conservatism and intolerance undermined the stability of Mughal society, while other historians question this, noting that he built Hindu temples, employed significantly more Hindus in his imperial bureaucracy than his predecessors did, opposed bigotry against Hindus and Shia Muslims.

- **Aurangzeb's son, Bahadur Shah I**

Aurangzeb's son, Bahadur Shah I, repealed the religious policies of his father and attempted to reform the administration. "However, after his death in 1712, the Mughal dynasty sank into chaos and violent feuds. In 1719 alone, four emperors successively ascended the throne", as figureheads under the rule of the Indian Muslim Sayyid king-makers.

During the reign of Muhammad Shah (reigned 1719–1748), the empire began to break up, and vast tracts of central India passed from Mughal to Maratha hands. As the Mughals tried to suppress the independence of the Nizam in the Deccan, he encouraged the Marathas to invade central and northern India. The far-off Indian campaign of Nader Shah, who had previously reestablished Iranian suzerainty over most of West Asia, the Caucasus, and Central Asia, culminated with the Sack of Delhi and shattered the remnants of Mughal power and prestige. Many of the empire's elites now sought to control their own affairs, and broke away to form indcpendent kingdoms. But, according to Sugata Bose and Ayesha Jalal, the Mughal Emperor continued to be the highest manifestation of sovereignty. Not only the Muslim gentry, but the Maratha, Hindu, and Sikh leaders took part in ceremonial acknowledgments of the emperor as the sovereign of India.Meanwhile, some regional polities within the increasingly fragmented Mughal Empire, involved themselves and the state in global conflicts, leading only to defeat and loss of territory during the Carnatic Wars and the Bengal War.

- **The remnants of the empire in 1751**

The Mughal Emperor Shah Alam II (1759–1806) made futile attempts to reverse the Mughal decline but ultimately had to seek the protection of the Emir of Afghanistan, Ahmed Shah Abdali, which led to the Third Battle of Panipat between the Maratha Empire and the Afghans (led by Abdali) in 1761. In 1771, the Marathas recaptured Delhi from Afghan control and in 1784 they officially became the protectors of the emperor in Delhi, a state of affairs that continued until the Second Anglo-Maratha War. Thereafter, the British East India Company became the protectors of the Mughal dynasty in Delhi.

The British East India Company took control of the former Mughal province of Bengal-Bihar in 1793 after it abolished local rule (Nizamat) that lasted until 1858, marking the beginning of British colonial era over the Indian subcontinent. By 1857 a considerable part of former Mughal India was under the East India Company's control. After a crushing defeat in the war of 1857–1858 which he nominally led, the last Mughal, Bahadur Shah Zafar, was deposed by the British East India Company and exiled in 1858. Through the Government of India Act 1858 the British Crown assumed direct control of East India Company-held territories in India in the form of the new British Raj. In 1876 the British Queen Victoria assumed the title of Empress of India.

Historians have offered numerous explanations for the rapid collapse of the Mughal Empire between 1707 and 1720, after a century of growth and prosperity. In fiscal terms, the throne lost the revenues needed to pay its chief officers, the emirs (nobles) and their entourages. The emperor lost authority, as the widely scattered imperial officers lost confidence in the central authorities, and made their own deals with local men of influence. The imperial army, bogged down in long, futile wars against the more aggressive Marathas, lost its fighting spirit. Finally came a series of violent political feuds over control of the throne. After the execution of Emperor Farrukhsiyar in 1719, local Mughal successor states took power in region after region.Contemporary chroniclers bewailed the decay they witnessed, a theme picked up by the first British historians who wanted to underscore the need for a British-led rejuvenation.

- **Since the 1970s**

Since the 1970s historians have taken multiple approaches to the decline, with little consensus on which factor was dominant. The psychological interpretations emphasise depravity in high places, excessive luxury, and increasingly narrow views that left the rulers unprepared for an external challenge. A Marxist school (led by Irfan Habib and based at Aligarh Muslim University) emphasises excessive exploitation of the peasantry by the rich, which stripped away the will and the means to support the regime. Karen Leonard has focused on the failure of the regime to work with Hindu bankers, whose financial support was increasingly needed; the bankers then helped the Maratha and the British. In a religious interpretation, some scholars argue that the Hindu powers revolted against the rule of a Muslim dynasty. Finally, other scholars argue that the very prosperity of the Empire inspired the provinces to achieve a high degree of independence, thus weakening the imperial court.

Jeffrey G. Williamson has argued that the Indian economy went through deindustrialization in the latter half of the 18th century as an indirect outcome of the collapse of the Mughal Empire, with British rule later causing further deindustrialization. According to Williamson, the decline of the Mughal Empire led to a decline in agricultural productivity, which drove up food prices, then nominal wages, and then textile prices, which led to India losing a share of the world textile market to Britain even before it had superior factory technology. Indian textiles, however, still maintained a competitive advantage over British textiles up until the 19th century.

- **Government of the Mughal Empire**

The Mughal Empire had a highly centralised, bureaucratic government, most of which was instituted during the rule of the third Mughal emperor Akbar. The central government was headed by the Mughal emperor immediately beneath him were four ministries. The finance/revenue ministry was responsible for controlling revenues from the empire's territories, calculating tax revenues, and using this information to distribute assignments. The ministry of the military was headed by an official titled mir bakhshi, who was in charge of military organisation, messenger service, and the mansabdari system. The ministry in charge of law/ religious patronage was the responsibility of the sadr as-sudr, who appointed judges and managed charities and stipends. Another ministry was dedicated to the imperial household and public works.

The empire was divided into suba (provinces), each of which were headed by a provincial governor called a subadar. The structure of the central government was mirrored at the provincial level; each suba had its own bakhshi, sadr as-sudr, and finance minister that reported directly to the central government rather than the subahdar. Subas were subdivided into administrative units known as sarkars, which were further divided into groups of villages known as parganas. Mughal government in the pargana consisted of a Muslim judge and local tax collector.

The Mughals had multiple imperial capitals, established over the course of their rule. These were the cities of Agra, Delhi, Lahore, and Fatehpur Sikri. Power often shifted back and forth between these capitals. Sometimes this was necessitated by political and military demands, but shifts also occurred for ideological reasons , or even simply because the cost of establishing a new capital was marginal. Situations where there were two simultaneous capitals happened multiple times in Mughal history. Certain cities also served as short-term, provincial capitals, as was the case with Aurangzeb's shift to Aurangabad in the Deccan. Kabul was the summer capital of mughals from 1526 to 1681.

The imperial camp, used for military expeditions and royal tours, also served as a kind of mobile, "de-facto" administrative capital. From the time of Akbar, Mughal camps were huge in scale, accompanied by numerous personages associated with the royal court, as well as soldiers and labourers. All administration and governance was carried out within them. The Mughal Emperors spent a significant portion of their ruling period within these camps.After Aurangzeb, the Mughal capital definitively became the walled city of Shahjahanabad (today Old Delhi).

- **Delhi under Bahadur Shah II, 1842**

The Mughal Empire's legal system was context-specific and evolved over the course of the empire's rule. Being a Muslim state, the empire employed fiqh (Islamic jurisprudence) and therefore the fundamental institutions of Islamic law such as those of the qadi (judge), mufti (jurisconsult), and muhtasib (censor and market supervisor) were well-established in the Mughal Empire. However, the dispensation of justice also depended on other factors, such as administrative rules, local customs, and political convenience. This was due to Persianate influences on Mughal ideology, and the fact that the Mughal Empire governed a non-Muslim majority.

The Mughal Empire followed the Sunni Hanafi system of jurisprudence. In its early years, the empire relied on Hanafi legal references inherited from its predecessor, the Delhi Sultanate. These included the al-Hidayah (the best guidance) and the Fatawa al-Tatarkhaniyya (religious decisions of the Emire Tatarkhan). During the Mughal Empire's peak, the Fatawa 'Alamgiri was commissioned by Emperor Aurangzeb. This compendium of Hanafi law sought to serve as a central reference for the Mughal state that dealt with the specifics of the South Asian context.The Mughal Empire also drew on Persianate notions of kingship. Particularly, this meant that the Mughal emperor was considered the supreme authority on legal affairs.

Various kinds of courts existed in the Mughal empire. One such court was that of the qadi. The Mughal qadi was responsible for dispensing justice; this included settling disputes, judging people for crimes, and dealing with inheritances and orphans. The qadi also had additional importance with regards to documents, as the seal of the qadi was required to validate deeds and tax records. Qadis did not constitute a single position, but made up a hierarchy. For example, the most basic kind was the pargana (district) qadi. More prestigious positions were those of the qadi al-quddat (judge of judges) who accompanied the mobile imperial camp, and the qadi-yi lashkar (judge of the army). Qadis were usually appointed by the emperor or the sadr-us-sudr (chief of charities). The jurisdiction of the qadi was availed by Muslims and non-Muslims alike.

The jagirdar (local tax collector) was another kind of official approached, especially for high-stakes cases. Subjects of the Mughal Empire also took their grievances to the courts of superior officials who held more authority and punitive power than the local qadi. Such officials included the kotwal (local police), the faujdar (an officer controlling multiple districts and troops of soldiers), and the most powerful, the subahdar (provincial governor). In some cases, the emperor themself dispensed justice directly. Jahangir was known to have installed a "chain of justice" in the Agra fort that any aggrieved subject could shake to get the attention of the emperor and bypass the inefficacy of officials.Self-regulating tribunals operating at the community or village level were common, but sparse documentation of them exists. For example, it is unclear how panchayats (village councils) operated in the Mughal era.

- **Economy of the Mughal Empire**

The Mughal economy was large and prosperous. During the Mughal era, the gross domestic product (GDP) of India in 1600 was estimated at 22% of the world economy, the second largest in the world, behind only China (Ming era) but larger than Europe. By 1700, the GDP of India had risen to 24% of the world economy, the largest in the world, larger than both China (Qing era) and Western Europe. India was producing 24.5% of the world's manufacturing output up until 1750. India's GDP growth increased over the

1500-1820 period, having grown faster than over the 1-1000 and 1000-1500 periods. India's economy has been described as a form of proto-industrialization, like that of 18th-century Western Europe prior to the Industrial Revolution.

The Mughals were responsible for building an extensive road system, creating a uniform currency, and the unification of the country.185–204 The empire had an extensive road network, which was vital to the economic infrastructure, built by a public works department set up by the Mughals which designed, constructed and maintained roads linking towns and cities across the empire, making trade easier to conduct.

- **Coin of Aurangzeb, minted in Kabul, dated 1691**

The Mughals adopted and standardised the rupee (rupiya, or silver) and dam (copper) currencies introduced by Sur Emperor Sher Shah Suri during his brief rule.The currency was initially 48 dams to a single rupee in the beginning of Akbar's reign, before it later became 38 dams to a rupee in the 1580s, with the dam's value rising further in the 17th century as a result of new industrial uses for copper, such as in bronze cannons and brass utensils. The dam was initially the most common coin in Akbar's time, before being replaced by the rupee as the most common coin in succeeding reigns. The dam's value was later worth 30 to a rupee towards the end of Jahangir's reign, and then 16 to a rupee by the 1660s. The Mughals minted coins with high purity, never dropping below 96%, and without debasement until the 1720s.

Despite India having its own stocks of gold and silver, the Mughals produced minimal gold of their own, but mostly minted coins from imported bullion, as a result of the empire's strong export-driven economy, with global demand for Indian agricultural and industrial products drawing a steady stream of precious metals into India. Around 80% of Mughal India's imports were bullion, mostly silver, with major sources of imported bullion including the New World and Japan, which in turn imported large quantities of textiles and silk from the Bengal Subah province.

Thank You

Thank You For Reading This Book And Shared This Book To Friends As Birthday Gift Have A Wonderfull Day.

Printed by Libri Plureos GmbH in Hamburg,
Germany